EUROPE WITH EURAIL 2024

An Essential Travel Guide To Explore Europe Trip By Train travel

Clara R. Burgher

TABLE OF CONTENTS

Sweden Tips and Tricks
Europe Train Trip for Foodies
Things I Wish I Had Understood Before Taking Eurail to Europe
TRAVEL JOURNAL

BONUS

(Turn to page 295)

INTRODUCTION

Your Easy Guide to Epic Train Adventures

Get ready to explore Europe like a pro with our simple yet comprehensive guide, "Europe with Eurail 2024." Discover hidden gems, immerse yourself in diverse cultures, and experience the magic of Europe's rail network.

Board Europe's extensive rail network and let the tracks carry you away. Imagine gliding through stunning landscapes, traversing snow-capped mountains, and coasting along sunny coastlines. With Eurail, you'll have the freedom to travel at your own pace, making the most of every moment.

From the charming streets of Paris to the vibrant piazzas of Rome, each city in Europe has a unique story to tell. Immerse yourself in Florence's art scene, wander through Venice's enchanting canals, and marvel at the architectural masterpieces that adorn every corner of the continent.

With Eurail, you'll forget about the stress of navigating unfamiliar cities and car rentals. Simply hop on a train, relax in your comfortable seat, and let the world unfold before you. Change your itinerary as you please, allowing spontaneity to guide your adventure.

"Europe with Eurail 2024" is your passport to a world of endless possibilities. Discover hidden gems off the beaten path, savor local delicacies, and forge unforgettable connections with fellow travelers along the way.

The time to explore Europe is now, and Eurail is your key to unlocking its boundless treasures. With "Europe with Eurail 2024" as your guide, you'll craft an itinerary that reflects your wanderlust and create memories that will last a lifetime.

Don't let this opportunity slip away. Secure your Eurail pass today and embark on the adventure of a lifetime.

What is a travel day?

A travel day is a 24-hour period during which you can use your Eurail Pass to travel by train. It lasts from 12:00 AM (midnight) until 11:59 PM on the same calendar day. You can use the train networks where your Eurail Pass is valid on each trip day.

Traveling from one European city to the next should take no more than one day on average. For example, you can go from Berlin to Amsterdam in one day and from Amsterdam to Paris the next.

A travel day for mobile passes runs from 00:00 (midnight) to 23:59 Central European Time (CET). Please keep in mind that several European countries do not follow CET. Finland, Estonia, Latvia, Lithuania, Romania, Bulgaria, and Greece are all one hour ahead (CET+1). This implies that there may be a difference in the start and finish times of a travel day when compared to your local time when traveling.

With a Continuous Pass, such as the 1 Month Continuous Pass, every day of the validity period is a travel day, so you can travel by train every day if you choose! A Flexi Pass, such as the 5 Days in 1 Month Pass, allows you to select which days you wish to travel up to the number indicated.

Night Trains

When traveling on a night train that departs one day and arrives the next, without changing trains after midnight, you only have to spend one travel day: the day of departure. If you change trains after midnight, you must spend two days traveling. You cannot use your Eurail Pass to catch a night train on your last travel day since the validity period expires at 23.59.

Night Ferries

When traveling on an overnight ferry covered by your Pass, you only need to utilize one travel day: the day of departure (note: the ferry's departure and arrival days must fall within the validity of the Pass). You do not need to utilize a travel day if you are using a cheap boat route.

What is a Eurail Pass?

The Eurail Pass is a single train pass that allows you to travel as much as you like on participating European train networks for a fixed number of travel days. There are many validity periods to pick from, ranging from 4 travel days to a maximum of 3 months.

You may travel with a Eurail Global Pass, which is valid in 33 European countries, or one of the Eurail One Country Passes.

The majority of the Passes, including the Eurail Global Pass, are now accessible as a smartphone Pass.

Eurail Passes may only be used by non-European nationals or residents. Instead, Europeans may utilize an Interrail Pass.

Do I need a Eurail or Interrail Pass?

Non-European citizens or residents may only use a Eurail Pass. Instead, European residents can purchase an Interrail Pass for the same price as a Eurail Pass from Interrail.eu.

If you are not a European citizen but are a legal resident of Europe, you may also utilize an Interrail Pass. They do ask for your country of residence when you order, so bring a proper European residency card or documents that match the country of residence mentioned on your Interrail Pass with you.

Note: If you are a national of a country outside the EU and want to visit or travel inside the EU, you will need a valid passport and perhaps a visa. Your passport must be valid for at least three months after the day you want to exit the EU.

If you hold more than one passport or permanent residence (dual citizenship), the Pass you use will be determined by where you live:
1. If you have both a European and a non-European passport, use the passport/ID of the country in which you reside. If you reside outside of Europe, get a Eurail Pass. If you reside in Europe, visit Interrail.eu to purchase an Interrail Pass.
2. If you hold a European passport and a non-European passport but live in a separate European nation, you may travel with any passport/ID, but your county of residence is the one in which you live. Order an Interrail Pass and provide an official residence card or paperwork, as well as your passport/ID.
3. If you have two European passports, you must always use an Interrail Pass from Interrail.eu. Order your Pass using the passport/ID of the country in which you reside.

Please keep in mind that a driver's license is not a suitable travel document.

Which Eurail Pass should I get?

Which Pass you should pick is determined first and primarily by your destination. If you just want to visit one country, you may get a One Country Pass for that country. If you wish to visit numerous countries, the Global Pass (valid in 33 European countries) is your best choice.

Second, pick a Pass that corresponds to the number of days you want to utilize the European rail network. These so-called travel days are available in a variety of lengths, ranging from four days to three months.

Finally, if you want a bit more comfort and elegance, a 1st class Pass is the way to go. If you're on a tight budget or don't care about luxury, 2nd class is the more cost-effective way to visit everything on your itinerary.

Finally, you may travel using a smartphone Pass or a paper Pass. A mobile Pass eliminates the need for paper and eliminates the need to wait for delivery; Eurail will give you everything by e-mail. This makes it an excellent choice if you want to get started traveling straight away. If you prefer to travel with a paper Pass, choose 'paper Pass' at the checkout. For the paper Pass, shipping times vary by country, so be sure to check the anticipated delivery time at checkout.

How can I purchase a Eurail Pass?

You may purchase your Eurail Pass online, and the activation number will be sent to you.
After purchasing your pass, all you need to do is download the Rail Planner app, activate your Pass using the code you'll get via email within 24 hours, and you're ready to board your first train!

What if you still prefer a paper pass?

Eurail has transitioned to totally digital passes, and I strongly advise you to use the online pass rather than a paper ticket, but you still have the option of going to old school.

In such a scenario, you should purchase the Eurail pass while still in your home country, with enough time before your travel to obtain the pass by mail.

The Eurail passes may be shipped to your hotel, If you're already in Europe. Simply notify the personnel at your hotel or hostel that you are expecting a package.

Continue to the checkout and complete your address data to get information on delivery costs and how long it will take for your Passes to arrive.

Passes are sent to addresses all across the globe, including Europe.

Your house, workplace, hotel, or hostel. All passes are shipped by registered mail, so please make sure someone is present to sign for your item when it comes. It doesn't matter who signs for the shipment.

Military APO addresses. Delivery to your army base takes an extra 4 weeks.

PO Box addresses are used in several countries.

The pass may be purchased eleven months to a week before your travel. I suggest getting it at least a month in advance and always factor in delivery time to your destination.

After purchasing a rail pass, you have eleven months to activate it at a train station in Europe.

Since 2019, you may now pre-activate your paper Eurail pass online. To do so, just choose the "activate my pass" option at the Eurail checkout when placing your purchase.

The mobile pass is activated the minute you use the planning app.

While it is preferable to purchase the passes online, certain major European train stations sell select Global Passes, albeit at a significantly higher price than online. Some nations also sell their own local passes at important stations, although at a higher price.

How To Use The Eurail Pass

How do you activate your Eurail Pass?

You must activate your pass online or via the Rail App, Before you board your first train.

If you use a paper pass, you must activate it at a train station in a nation where Eurail is valid.

When you activate a paper pass, a train official will fill in the start and end dates of your pass, as well as your passport number.

They will also stamp your pass to authenticate the start date of your train journey.

Within eleven months, activation is necessary after the issuance date. To activate, you have to provide ID (passport) and the pass.

Eurail now allows you to pre-activate your pass when you buy it. Simply choose the "activate my pass" option at checkout when placing your transaction.

Learn from my mistake: I activated my pass in Athens, where I began my journey, but I didn't realize that they didn't stamp it. It wasn't until I was on the sleeper train from Bucharest to Budapest that the train conductor noticed the absence of a stamp, thus I had to pay the full ticket for that trip and activate the pass (again) in Budapest. (The activation is free).

Does Eurail provide any discounts?

Yes, Eurail offers the following discounts on Eurail Passes every year:

- **Youth Pass -** Travelers aged 12 to 27 can purchase a Youth Pass, saving 23% off typical Adult Pass pricing.

- **A family pass** allows up to two children (ages 0 to 11) to travel for free with a single adult.

- **Adults 60** and over get a 10% discount on standard Adult Pass pricing.

Is the Eurostar included in my Eurail Pass?

Yes! If you have a Eurail Global Pass, you may travel on the Eurostar high-speed train that connects London to France, Belgium, and the Netherlands.

Seat reservations are required for this train and may be requested up to 6 months in advance.

What are seat reservations?

A seat reservation is a ticket that guarantees you a seat on a certain train, even if it's highly crowded. Reservations are required for most high-speed trains and all night trains in Europe.

Please keep in mind that reservations are charged by European train operators. Your Eurail Pass does not cover them.

Which trains need seat reservations?

Most high-speed trains and all night trains in Europe need a reservation. Reservations are often needed in France, Italy, and Spain. Trains in these nations are popular and rapidly fill up, particularly during the summer months.

Many other nations, such as Austria, the Benelux, and Germany, allow you to travel without making reservations.

Countries with minimal reservations

If you want completely spontaneous travel, these nations are your best choice, since most domestic trains do not need any reservations at all! If you really want to, you can generally still book a reservation.

- Belgium Austria
- Germany
- Ireland Luxembourg
- Montenegro
- Netherlands
- Slovakia
- Turkey

Countries having a high number of reservations

Because the railroads in these popular nations serve large numbers of passengers every day, many of their trains need reservations. You may need to prepare ahead of time, but the many high-speed connections on some of Europe's quickest trains allow you to see more in less time!

- France
- Greece
- Italy
- Spain

Countries with reservations

In these places, advanced planning goes a long way! Some trains need reservations, while others do not.
- Bosnia and Herzegovina
- Bulgaria
- Croatia
- Czech Republic

- Denmark
- Finland
- Hungary
- Norway
- Poland
- Portugal
- Romania
- Serbia
- Slovenia Sweden
- Switzerland

Seat ticket Fees Determine how much you need to spend for seat reservations if you want to travel by high-speed domestic or international trains, or if you need to get a ticket for a night train.

High-speed trains
- Speed between cities in the same nation
- Reservations are sometimes required for extra speed and comfort.
- The average price is €10.

International high-speed trains
- Speed across borders
- Reservations are sometimes required for extra speed and comfort.
- The average price is €15.

Night trains
- While sleeping, you can travel vast distances.
- Reserve a seat, bunk, or couchette
- Reservations are almost usually required.
- The average price is €20.

Why do I have to pay for reservations?

Seat reservations are not included in your Eurail Pass; they are an extra payment imposed by several train operators to ensure that everyone gets a seat on crowded services.

It may seem to be a lot on top of the cost of your Pass, but trains that need necessary reservations usually save you a lot of time and offer lots of added facilities like internet and power outlets, so you can kick back and relax as you race to your next location.

If you're traveling on a budget, keep in mind that most slower national and regional trains don't need seat reservations, so if you're prepared to take the scenic way, you can frequently save the additional fee.

How do I reserve seats?

With your Eurail Pass, you may jump on and off trains as you choose, however, certain services may need you to purchase an extra seat reservation. Seat reservations are not included in your Eurail Pass, but for a charge, they guarantee you a comfortable seat on the busiest routes across Europe. Seat reservations are required on all high-speed trains and all night trains.

You may reserve your reservations with Eurail in three simple steps:

1. Purchase your pass
First and foremost, decide which Pass you will use to tour Europe.

2. Plan your route
Choose where you want to travel and see whether you need to secure a seat.

3. Make your reservations.
With the Eurail online service, you can book your seat reservations quickly and conveniently.

Night Trains

Can you sleep on the Eurail train?

Yes, Night train traveling across Europe is also a once-in-a-lifetime event. When you reserve a bed (sleeper or couchette), a sheet, blanket, and pillow are normally included. However, Please keep in mind that if you cross a border by night train, you will very certainly be required to provide your Interrail pass and passport to the train conductor.

What is the difference between a couchette and a sleeper on Eurail?

Sleepers feature a bed and, in most cases, a private washbasin, towels, and bed linen, and can seat up to four people in single, double, or three-person compartments. Couchettes are inexpensive overnight accommodations that accommodate up to six guests on bunk beds and provide a pillow and blanket.

What is the 7 p.m. rule?

Here's how the 7 p.m. rule works.

If your overnight train departs after 7 p.m., you can enter the next day's date on your rail pass and utilize one rather than two days of travel for the overnight journey. Simple!

What is the train sleeping rule?

You can only sleep in your berth from 10 p.m. until 6 a.m. However ,You are not permitted to sleep in your berth for more than this number of hours. If you do, your co-passenger with a lower berth may stop you.
Are sleeper trains worthwhile?

Overnight rail routes are becoming increasingly smarter alternatives to cars and planes, turning the journey to your destination into an experience in itself.

Do overnight trains count as two days on the Eurail Pass? Night trains

When traveling on a night train that departs one day and arrives the next, without changing trains after midnight, you only have to spend one travel day: the day of departure. If you change trains after midnight, you must spend two days traveling.

Method To Sleep On A Train

8 Tips for sleeping overnight

1. Choose Your Seat Wisely.
   Your trip starts with selecting the appropriate sleeping position.
2. Bring a Neck Pillow
3. ear Comfortable Clothing (and shoes)
4. Pack Earplugs and an Eye Mask
5. Bring a Blanket.
6. Travel with a Friend
7. Bring Your Own Snacks and Water
8. Adjust Your Seat.

Do European trains have showers?

Sleepers, couchettes, and seats are the three forms of accommodation available on European sleeper trains. Sleepers provide mattresses with all essential bedding in one, two, or three-bed compartments, with all compartments including a washbasin and, on certain routes, a tiny private shower and toilet.

What are European sleeper trains like?

Sleeper cabins

At night, beds are newly prepared with pillows, duvets, or blankets. Sleeper cabins often have a sink, towels, and toiletries, allowing you to arrive at your destination as refreshed as possible. Some luxury sleeping suites also include their own shower and toilet for complete privacy throughout your vacation.

Accommodation

WHERE TO SLEEP ON TRAVELS

Where to sleep on a train journey (Interrail, Eurail).

- Hostels
- hotels
- night trains, and
- camping are all options for lodging.

Where to book

- Booking.com and Airbnb

European Rail Trip on A Budget

- Think beyond the big city stops.
  - When it comes to European train travel, the major cities - Paris, Amsterdam, Barcelona, Rome, and Berlin - are usually at the top of the list. However, thanks to Europe's regional rail network, you don't have to stick to the famous (and frequently crowded and pricey) stops.

- Take the scenic rail route and sleep on the train
- Check out rail passes
  - (but don't assume they'll be cheaper)
- Book in advance
- Know who to book with: Third-party firms such as Omio and Trainline offer tickets for trips all around Europe.
- Pack a picnic
  - So, to avoid having to purchase costly train meals and to avoid being hungry, prepare a picnic to eat on board. Most major train stations have shops, but there is generally a larger supermarket nearby where you can fill up on food and drink.

Spain

The majority of trains on the Spanish rail network are operated by RENFE, the country's national train operator. Spain is linked to the rest of Europe via high-speed and night trains. Spanish train timetables may be found on the Eurail timetable as well as the RENFE website.

Route Maps

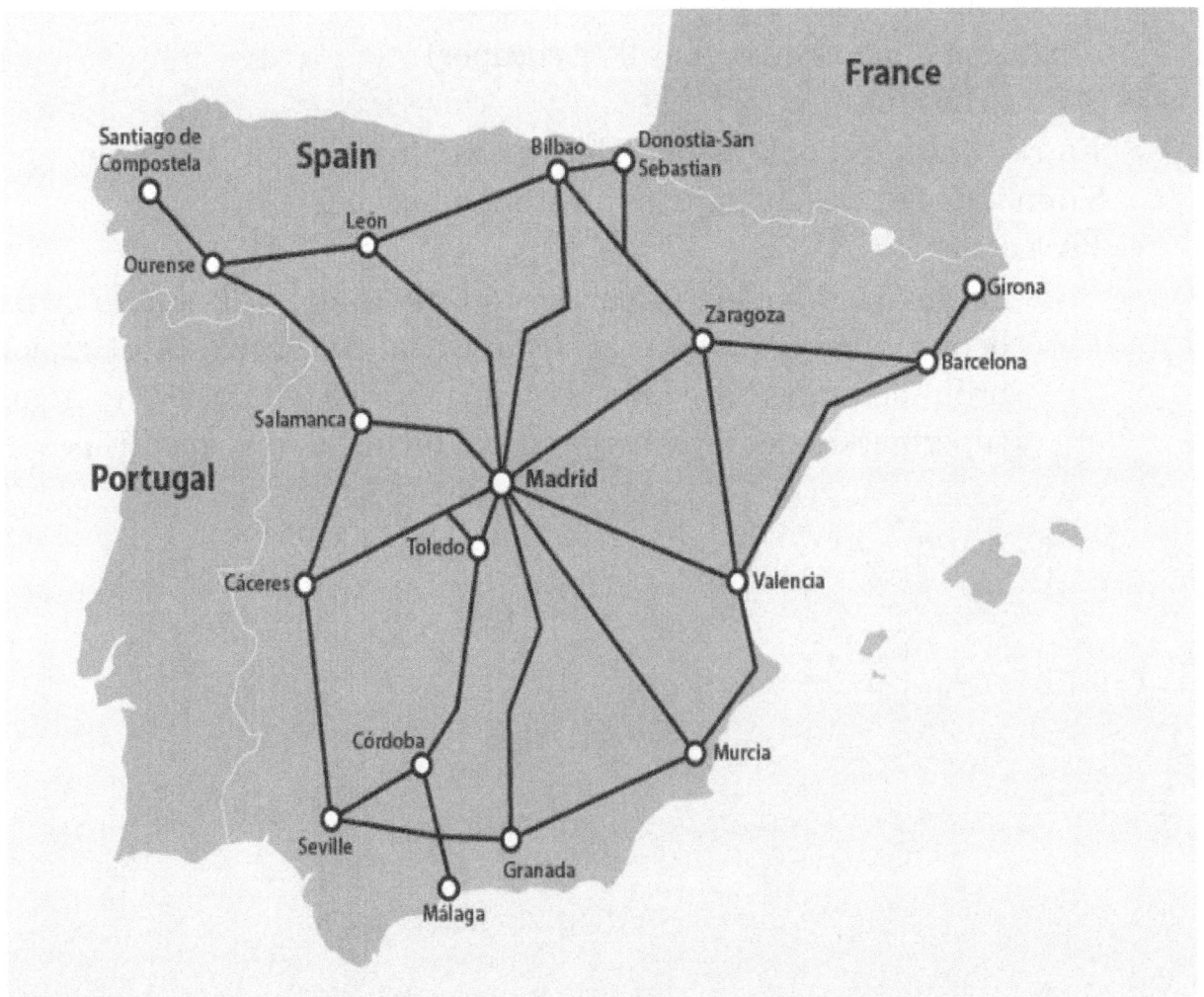

Train Types in Spain

• Domestic train
Regional and intercity trains
Media Distancia (RE)
- Connects bigger cities with smaller locations across medium distances.
- Fast trains make many stops throughout their routes.

Cercanas (RE)
- Suburban trains that serve Spain's major cities such as Madrid and Valencia. In Catalonia, near Barcelona, these trains are known as Rodalies.

Domestic high-speed trains
Avant (AVN)
- High-speed services for short travels on short to medium routes.
- Faster and more comfortable than Media Distancia with comparable coverage.

AVE (AVE)
- These trains move at speeds of up to 310 km/h (193 mph) throughout Europe's largest high-speed rail network.
- It takes less than 3 hours to go from Madrid to Barcelona.

Alvia (ALV)
- Trains are comfortable, long-distance trains that link Madrid and Barcelona to locations across Spain.

Intercity (IC)
- Trains are comfortable, long-distance trains that link Madrid with locations in southern Spain.

Euromed (EUR)

- Trains are high-speed, air-conditioned trains that travel along the Mediterranean coast of north-eastern Spain.
- Connects significant cities in the Levante region: Barcelona to Valencia in little over 3 hours, then on to Alicante.

International high-speed trains in Spain
TGV INOUI to France

- TGV INOUI trains are operated by French railroads.
- Barcelona to Paris.

RENFE AVE to France

- Barcelona - Lyon
- Madrid - Marseille
- Reservations are necessary.

Celta (IC)

- Intercity trains that connect Vigo Guixar in Spain with Porto in Portugal.

International Trains
Other International Routes to France
Rodalies (RE)

Local trains from Barcelona may take you to places such as Perpignan and Toulouse. As an alternative to direct Barcelona-Paris services, these French cities are well linked to Paris and the rest of France by TGV and other trains.

- Barcelona - Latour de Carol (France),
(search for La Tor de Querol-Enveitg).

Connecting trains run to Toulouse from Latour de Carol.
See the schedule and filter on regional trains for Barcelona-Cerbère (France).

Connecting trains run from Cerbere to Perpignan, Montpellier, Nîmes, and Avignon in France.

Alvia (ALV) Madrid - Irun
Madrid - Valladolid - San Sebastian - Irun
(French border).
- A 3km walk from Irun to Hendaye (France) for direct trains to Bordeaux and Paris. Take the Euskotren (not included for Passholders).

Other international routes to Portugal
IC & Regional train (RE)
- Madrid - Lisbon/Porto (Portugal).
    Madrid to Badajoz by IC
     Badajoz - Entroncamento.
    Entroncamento - Lisbon/Porto with connecting trains

Night Trains
Intercités de Nuit (NT)
Night trains that link Spain and France. The following routes are beneficial for visitors visiting France:
- Latour de Carol - Paris (ICN 3974/3975) - Open daily all year.
- Cerbere - Paris (ICN 3730/3731) - Only on Fridays and Sundays till June 30th. Every day throughout the summer.
- Hendaye - Paris (ICN 3741/3742) - Daily from July 7th until September 2nd.

Use the Intercités de Nuit as an alternate way to France.
Night trains from Latour de Carol and Hendaye are viable alternatives to the busy TGV lines from Barcelona. The night train to Hendaye is a viable option for getting to San Sebastian and Bilbao.
- Search for Latour de Carol to Paris in our schedule and the local train from Barcelona to Latour de Carol on the Rodalies website ('La Tor de Querol-Enveitg').

- In the timetable, look for Cerbere to Paris and Barcelona to Cerbere in separate searches. During the summer, this train only travels once a day.
- Find the local trains from San Sebastian and Bilbao on Euskotren* to Spain by searching for Hendaye to Paris in the timetable. Trains from San Sebastian and Madrid arrive at Irun, which is a 30-minute walk or a 4-minute rail trip over the border.

*Euskotren is not part of the Eurail network. Purchase your tickets at Hendaye from vending machines or at the ticket counter.

Domestic Connection

Here are estimated travel times between Spain's most popular cities when traveling direct high-speed trains.

Route	Duration
Barcelona to Madrid (AVE high-speed train)	2h 30m
Barcelona to Malaga (AVE high-speed train)	2h 30m
Madrid to Granada (AVE high-speed train)	3h 35m
Madrid to Valencia (AVE high-speed train)	1h 50m

Madrid to Santiago de Compostela (Alvia high-speed train)	3h 15m
Madrid to Seville (AVE high-speed train)	2h 30m
Barcelona to Valencia (Euromed high-speed train)	2h 50m
Madrid to Irun (Alvia high-speed train)	5h 50m

You do not need to make reservations when traveling on slower regional trains. For example, a direct regional rail travel from Barcelona to Madrid takes 9h 06m. That is 6 and a half hours longer than the high-speed rail route.

INTERNATIONAL Connections

Popular European cities from which to travel to and from Spain include:

Route	Which train?	Duration	Reservations

Barcelona to Paris (France)	SNCF	6h 50m	Required
Vigo to Porto (Portugal)	Celta	2h 15m	Required
Madrid to Lisbon (Portugal) via Badajoz	IC + RE + IC	9h	Required (Madrid – Badajoz & Entroncament o – Lisbon)
Madrid to Porto (Portugal) via Badajoz	IC + RE + IC	11h	Required (Madrid – Badajoz & Entroncament o – Lisbon)
Madrid to Porto (Portugal) via Vigo	ALV + RE + IC	11h	Required (Madrid – Pontevedra)

Reservations

How can I book rail tickets in Spain?

Most trains in Spain need advanced bookings. Fees vary based on the type of seat or bed you choose.

Eurail reservation self-service system

- Eurail
- TGV Barcelona-Paris (international tickets only)
- Only AVE, Euromed, and Alvia trains operate.

At a local train station

Reservations for other domestic and long-distance trains in Spain can only be made locally at a Spanish Long Distance railway station's ticket counter. Here is a list of long-distance rail stations.Reservations can be made on the day of travel or up to 3 months in advance.

International TGVs linking Barcelona with Lyon and Paris in France can only be booked at train stations in France and via the Eurail reservation self-service system.

By calling RENFE

- phone sales +34 91 232 03 20
- It is possible to reserve a seat ahead of time. You will be given a PNR number, which you must use to pick up and pay for your reservation at a local station ticket office, while displaying your Eurail Pass. You must collect your reservation within 72 hours of booking. Reservations may only be made up to 24 hours before the train's departure time. The pre-reservation will expire after this period.
- Please keep in mind that a pre-reservation is not the same as a reservation. It just holds a seat for you for 72 hours.

If you have a handicap or limited mobility and wish to travel by rail in Spain, you may contact Atendo Service. You may reach them via phone:

- +34 91 214 05 05
- Availability: 24 hours a day, and seven days a week

Other places

- The following stations in Portugal have international ticket booths where you could make reservations for RENFE trains leaving from Badajoz and Vigo: Lisbon Santa Apolónia, Lisbon Oriente, Lisbon Rossio, Porto Campanha, Porto So Bento, Aveiro, Coimbra, and Faro.
- At a Deutsche Bahn ticket counter. You must specify the train number.
- Call Deutsche Bahn at (+49 30 2970 or +49 30 311682904). Collect at a DB ticket machine or receive by mail (€5.90 per order). You must specify the train number.
- via a Swiss ticket office or by phone

Spain Pass

- Spend your whole holiday exploring Spain by train.
- Prices start at $ 169 for the

Global Pass

- Have the flexibility to travel to Spain and up to 32 more European countries.
- Standard pricing begin at $ 211.

Quick Facts of Spain

- Madrid is the capital city.
- Population: 47.2 million
- Language: Spanish
- Euro (EUR)
- Dialing code: +34

The spelling of city names

On Spanish rail schedules and at Spanish train stations, you'll normally discover the local spelling of Spanish towns and stations.

Here is the local spelling of several well-known Spanish cities:
- Alicante = Alacant
- Seville = Sevilla

Spanish hub stations

The major hub stations in Spain are Madrid Puerta de Atocha-Almudena Grandes, Barcelona Sants, Irun, and Portbou. Trains to Spain's major cities and numerous overseas locations may be boarded at these rail stations.

Station Facilities

Stations in Spain often offer good amenities, which frequently include:
- Luggage Lockers
- Foreign exchange desks
- Restaurants and cafés
- Tourist information offices
- ATM cash machines
- Elevators and escalators
- Access for travelers with disabilities

Gates at stations for some local lines

Some local lines have gates where a barcode paper or mobile pass cannot be used.

There are a handful of stations with entry gates. Customers can request that certain stations be opened by showing their pass (and, if required, a seat reservation). If there is no staff at the station, the gates will remain open or will open automatically.

France

Train types in France

SNCF runs the majority of the French railway network.

Route maps

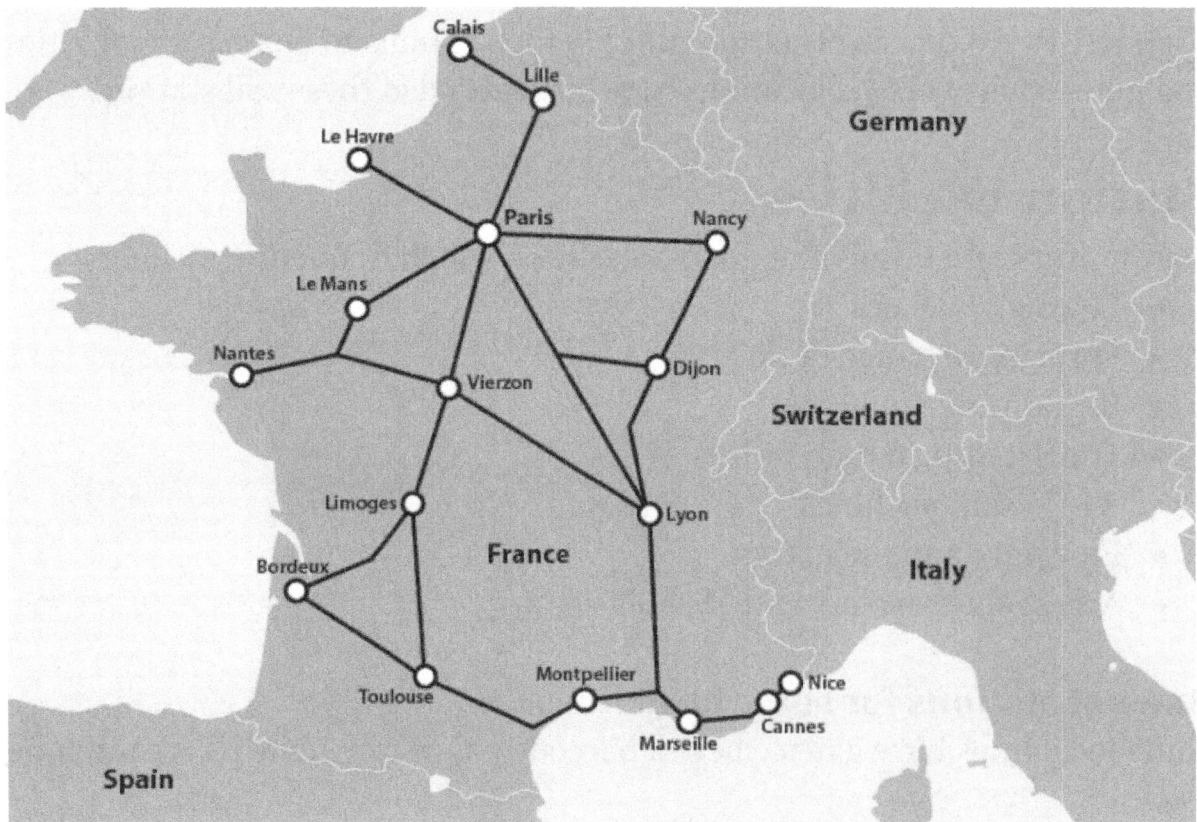

Domestic trains

Regional and intercity trains in France

Regional train reservations are not needed (except for TER services)

TER

- With regular services, it connects most French cities and towns.

- TER trains in Normandy (€1.5 reservation fee, payable only at train stations).

InterCité (InterCity)
- Connects France's largest cities and communities.
- The majority of InterCité trains do not need reservations.
- The SNCF website includes a map showing InterCité trains that need reservations (in French only: blue=reservations necessary; green=reservations not required; purple=night trains).

Suburban RER trains in Paris
RER trains link central Paris with the city's suburbs. Please keep in mind that certain trains are NOT covered in the Pass. Have this in mind before traveling to:
- Orly Airport
- Charles de Gaulle Airport
- Disneyland Paris
- Versailles

High-speed trains
Domestic high-speed trains in France
TGV
- Connects famous places like as Paris, Bordeaux, Lyon, Marseille, and Nice.
- Travels at 320 km/h (200 mph).
- The restaurant cars have luggage racks, electrical sockets, and refreshments.
- Reservations are necessary.

International high-speed trains in France
Eurostar
- High-speed connections to the United Kingdom, Belgium, Germany, and the Netherlands are available via the following routes:

- Paris - London
- Paris - Brussels
- Paris - Brussels - Antwerp - Rotterdam - Amsterdam
- Paris - Brussels - Liège - Cologne - Düsseldorf - Dortmund
- Disneyland Paris - Brussels - Antwerp - Rotterdam - Amsterdam

- Reservations are required for certain trains, which might be completely booked. I suggest booking your reservation as soon as possible to prevent disappointment.
- Former Thalys trains in red provide services to Brussels, Amsterdam, and Dortmund.

TGV and ICE to Germany

Connects French towns to a variety of German locations, including:
  - Paris - Frankfurt, Freiburg, Stuttgart, and Munich (Germany)
  - Marseille - Frankfurt (Germany)
  - Bordeaux - Frankfurt (Germany) Saturdays 08 July - 26 August
  - Bordeaux - Freiburg (Germany) Saturdays 01 April - 02 September
  - Reservations are necessary.

TGV to Barcelona

- Connects Paris with Barcelona (Spain).
- Reservations are necessary.
- In the summer, it quickly sells out; as an alternative, take Intercités de Nuit to Latour de Carol or Cerbère.

RENFE AVE to Spain

- Lyon - Barcelona
- Marseille - Madrid
- Reservations are necessary.

TGV Lyria

Connects Paris to Geneva and Zurich (Switzerland).
Reservations are necessary.

TGV to Brussels
- Connects many French cities to Brussels (Belgium), including:
- Lille, Lyon, Marseille, Montpellier, Nantes, Rennes, and Strasbourg to Brussels.
- Reservations are necessary.

TGV to Luxembourg
- Connects Montpellier to Luxembourg City (Luxembourg) and Paris
- Reservations are necessary.

TGV to Italy
- Connects Paris to Turin and Milan (Italy).
- Reservations are necessary.

Bordering nations' train station
An Interrail Pass valid in France permits you to travel to the following train stations in neighboring countries:
- Basel (Switzerland)
- Geneva (Switzerland)
- Portbou (Spain)
- Ventimiglia (Italy)

NIGHT TRAINS
Domestic night trains in France
Intercités de Nuit
Connects Paris to numerous places in France's east, west, and south:
- Paris - Toulouse (ICN 3731/3730
  or ICN 3751/3750) - Daily all year.
- Paris - Foix - Latour de Carol
  (ICN 3974/3975) - Daily all year.

- Paris - Toulouse - Perpignan - Cerbere (ICN 3730/3731) - Only on Fridays and Sundays till June 30th. Every day throughout the summer.

- Paris - Tarbes - Lourdes (ICN 3741/3742)
  - Daily all year.
- Paris - Rodez (ICN 3755/3756)
  - Just only on Sundays till the 25th of June.
- Paris - Marseille - Cannes - Nice
  (ICN 5771/5772) - Daily all year.
- Paris - Briançon (ICN 5789/5790) - Only on Sundays till June 18th.
- Paris - Lourdes - Biarritz - Hendaye (ICN 3741/3742) - Daily from July 7th to September 2nd.

Use the Intercités de Nuit as an alternate route to Spain.

Both the night trains to Latour de Carol and Cerbère are viable alternatives to the busy TGV route to Barcelona. The night train to Hendaye is a viable option for getting to San Sebastian and Bilbao.
- Search the Eurail timetable for Paris to Latour de Carol and the Rodalies website for the local train to Barcelona ('La Tor de Querol-Enveitg').
- In the Eurail timetable, search for Paris to Cerbere and Cerbere to Barcelona separately. During the summer, this train only operates every day.
- Find the local trains to San Sebastian and Bilbao on Euskotren (https://www.euskotren.eus/en) to Spain by searching for Paris to Hendaye in the Eurail schedule. RENFE trains to San Sebastian and Madrid leave at Irun, which is a 30-minute walk over the border or a 4-minute rail ride on Euskotren.

*Euskotren is not part of the Eurail network. Purchase your tickets at Hendaye from vending machines or the ticket counter.

Reservations are necessary for these trains.

International night trains in France
ÖBB Nightjet
- Paris - Munich - Vienna

Domestic routes

France has an enormous high-speed rail network that will get you where you want to go much quicker than the regional train system. However, on high-speed trains, you must make a seat reservation.

View estimated train travel times between major cities in France using regional and high-speed TGV trains:

Route	Regional	High-speed
Paris to Bordeaux	11h 30m	2h
Paris to Lyon	5h	2h
Paris to Marseille	10h 30m	3h
Paris to Nice	16h	5h 30m
Paris to Nantes	5h	2h 15m
Paris to Strasbourg	5h	1h 45m

Paris to Lille	3h		1h

International routes

Route	Which train?	Travel time	Reservations
Lyon to Geneva (Switzerland)	Regional	2h	None
Paris to Amsterdam (Netherlands)	Eurostar	3h 30m	Required
Paris to Brussels (Belgium)	Eurostar	1h 30m	Required
Paris to Cologne / Dortmund (Germany)	Eurostar	3h 30m / 5h	Required
Paris to London (Great Britain)	Eurostar	3h 30m	Required
Paris to Barcelona	TGV	6h 30m	Required

(Spain)

Paris to Munich (Germany)	TGV / ÖBB Nightjet	5h 30m / 11h (overnight)	Required
Paris to Frankfurt (Germany)	ICE & TGV	4h	Required
Paris to Geneva (Switzerland)	TGV	3h	Required
Nice to Genova / Milan (Italy)(via Ventimiglia)	Regional and InterCity	3h / 5h	Optional
Paris to Turin / Milan (Italy)	TGV	5h 30m / 7h	Required
Perpignan to Barcelona (Spain)	TGV	1h 30m	Required
Paris to Vienna (Austria)	ÖBB Nightjet	15h (overnight)	Required
Paris to Barcelona (Spain) via	Intercités de Nuit and Rodalies de	15h	Required only for Intercités de

Latour de Carol	<u>Catalunya</u>		Nuit
Paris to San Sebastian and Bilbao (Spain) via Hendaye	<u>TGV</u> or <u>Intercités de Nuit</u> to Hendaye and <u>Euskotren</u> to Spain	4h 40m / 13h 30m (overnight) to Hendaye	Required. Pass not valid on Euskotren

International ferry links to and from France

France to the United Kingdom

Get a 30% Eurail discount on Irish Ferries voyages from Rosslare in Ireland to Cherbourg (19.5 hours) or Roscoff (18.5 hours) in north-west France.

Irish Ferries routes

Irish Ferries operates the following ferry services between France, the Republic of Ireland, and Wales (Great Britain):

- Dublin - Cherbourg
- Dublin - Holyhead
- Pembroke - Rosslare

Services and Facilities

- Bar
- Café
- Children's play area
- Cinema
- Self-service restaurant
- Shops

Facilities may vary depending on the ferry and route.

Additional information

Prices and discounts for Eurail Pass holders

Irish Ferries offers Eurail Pass members a 30% discount on regular foot passenger rates (adult or kid). Cabin accommodations are available for an additional fee.

You are eligible for the discount if your Eurail Pass is valid in either the nation of departure or arrival. This discount does not require the use of a travel day on a flexi Pass. When you check in for the sailing, you may be requested to present your Eurail Pass.

Reservations

For all crossings, reservations are either required or highly suggested.

To book a reservation and get your discount, just follow these steps:

1. Pay in advance for a reservation at www.irishferries.com.

2. Send your booking reference number and Eurail Pass cover number to bookings@irishferries.com.

3. The applicable discount will be applied to your booking, and the credit will be reimbursed to you via the credit card system.

Before your departure date, send your email at least 5 days.

Travel time, number of crossings
Ireland- France

Overnight sailings. The sailing season is from February to December. There are no daily departures. Please confirm sailing schedules at www.irishferries.com.

Ireland - UK

Dublin - Holyhead: 3 hours 15 minutes (Dublin Swift 1 hour 49 minutes), 4 daily departures

Rosslare - Pembroke: 3 hours 45 minutes, 2 daily departures

Onboard facilities

To and from France

Cabaret Lounge, live onstage entertainment, family self-service restaurant, waiter service, restaurant, movie, gift shop, late-night disco, and for children: own performers, specialized play areas, special menus, and films. More information and contact information

For further information, visit www.irishferries.com/uk-en/frequently-asked-questions.

You can get aid or assistance from the following people:

Ireland
Dublin Head Office,
Alexandra Road, Ferryport, Dublin 1
Phone (+353) 818 300 400
E-mail: bookings@irishferries.com

Rosslare Harbour
Phone (+353) 53 913 3158

France
Cherbourg Gare Maritime
Phone (+33) 233234444

Reservations

Reservation system for Eurail
- Eurail
- TGV, ICE, Eurostar, Nightjet, Intercités de Nuit
- TGV to Barcelona

Booking via Eurail self-service costs administrative fees.
- EUR 2,- per person per train
- Additional € 9,- per order
- (for paper tickets)

With railway carriers
- B-Europe: Domestic Trains
    - TGV, Intercités, Intercités de Nuit
- SNCB (b-europe): International trains
    - TGV to Belgium and all Eurostar trains

By dialing SNCF
- +33 1 84 94 3635
- Select #85 for English.
- You may make both domestic and international bookings.
- The SNCF contact center presently only takes American Express payments.

Locally, vending machines are available in train stations in France.
- Domestic and some international trains are available at the station's SNCF ticket-selling machines. You may book the following international trains using SNCF ticket machines:
    - Accommodations and All Intercités de Nuit night train routes
    - Paris - Lausanne/Geneva (Switzerland)
    - Paris - Zurich (Switzerland)
    - Paris - Frankfurt/Stuttgart/Munich (Germany)
    - Paris - Milan/Turin (Italy)
    - Bordeaux - Frankfurt/Freiburg (Germany) (Seasonal)
    - Marseille - Frankfurt (Germany)
    - Paris - Barcelona (Spain)

Which trains in France need reservations?
- TGV high-speed trains
- TER trains in Normandy (€1.5 reservation charge, payable only at train stations)
- All international high-speed trains (such as Eurostar)
- All-night trains

Up to 3 months in advance reservations can be made. The number of seats available for Eurail Pass holders on the TGV, Eurostar trains, select

InterCité trains, and the Paris-Frankfurt ICE line is restricted. Please book your seats on these trains as long in advance as possible.

For more information on bookings for French trains, visit:

French trains with restricted seating for Eurail Pass holders

It's important to note that the number of seats available for Eurail Pass holders on the following trains is limited:

- TGV high-speed trains on international routes (excluding TGV Lyria)
- SNCF TGV Inoui high-speed trains to Barcelona
- InterCité trains
- InterCité de Nuit night trains
- ICE high-speed train on the lines Paris-Frankfurt, Paris-Munich, and Paris-Stuttgart.
- Eurostar is a high-speed train that connects London, Paris, Brussels, Amsterdam, and Dortmund.

I strongly advise you to book these trains as soon as possible. If you wait too long to reserve these reservations, the allocation of seats for Eurail Pass holders may be exhausted. Reservations for the aforementioned trains may be booked up to two months in advance.

Regional Trains in France

The train you wish to board may be completely booked, or you may want to avoid paying the extra reservation costs. In these instances, I suggest using regional trains that do not need reservations.

This means more train changes and longer trip durations, but it also allows you to view more of the lovely French countryside. It is not always easy to avoid trains with reservations, but it is always worth investigating. Simply click the 'No reservation required' option on the Eurail schedule.

Alternative routes for French trains

If the French train you wish to travel is full, you'll have to find another method to get to your destination. I investigated the top ten domestic and international rail lines in France. I illustrate the quickest method, which uses trains with restricted seats for pass holders, as well as various alternatives.

Please bear in mind that train times are approximate and include the time it takes to change trains.

Paris to Amsterdam
Paris to Barcelona
Paris to Brussels
Paris to Frankfurt
Marseille to Geneva
Paris to Milan
Paris to Zurich
Paris to Bordeaux
Paris to Marseille
Paris to Nice

Eurostar trains are popular and, as a result, frequently sell out rapidly. Make sure you obtain your seat reservation in advance.

France Pass

- Purchase your France Pass
- This pass enables you to travel across France!
- Prices start at $76.

Global Pass

- You are allowed to go to France and up to 32 other European countries.

- Standard pricing begins at $ 211.

France Tips and Techniques

Quick Facts

- Paris is the capital city.
- Population: 65 million
- Language: French
- Euro (EUR)
- dialing code: +33

Ferry Travel

A Eurail Pass valid in France on certain routes provides discounted ferry travel to Ireland.

- Roscoff - Rosslare (Ireland)
- Cherbourg - Rosslare (Ireland)

Additional advantages

Eurail Pass customers can get savings on a variety of accommodations, city cards, and even Disneyland!

Famous European Hostels

How can I take advantage of this promotion?

1. Purchase a Pass

First and foremost, decide which Pass you will use to tour Europe.
EITHER EURAIL PASSES OR INTERRAIL PASSES

2. Schedule your offer

To get your discount, go to www.famoushostels.com/eco-wanderer or use the calculator below to determine your CO_2 savings of up to 20% off your stay.

Who are Europe's Most Famous Hostels?

Who are we? Europe's Famous Hostels is an organization of 43 independently owned hostels. They have offices across Europe and Israel. The organization arose from a desire to promote one another and build a community in the hostel and travel sector, as well as to encourage sustainable travel across hostels.

What is an Eco-Wanderer?

The Eco-Wanderer campaign is an initiative centered on sustainable tourism. They created a Carbon Emissions calculator in collaboration with Eurail, which translates your CO_2 offset by choosing trains over airlines into direct discounts of up to 20% in our 43 hostels around Europe.

Highlights
How Does the CO2 Saver Calculator Work?

The procedure is really straightforward.

Log in to eco.famoushostels.com and input their starting point, any Famous Hostels destination from our list, and their discount by clicking on "Calculate my Offset."

Once you have your discount prediction, go into their portal using your Eurail/Interrail ticket and the reservation number from your reservation at one of our hostels.

Your conversion certificate (QR code) will be sent to you via email. Allowing you to authenticate at the reception of your preferred Famous Hostel and collect your discount.

Includes

- Flying Pig Uptown, Amsterdam
- Kabul, Barcelona
- ArkaBarka, Belgrade
- Sunflower Hostel, Berlin
- Latroupe La Granja, Bilbao
- Latroupe Grand Place, Brussels
- The Bauhaus, Bruges
- Maverick Hostel, Budapest

- Ostello Bello Lake Como, Como
- Copenhagen Downtown, Copenhagen
- St. Christophers, Edinburgh
- Wotel Surf Hostel, Ericeira
- Ostello Bello, Florence
- Five Elements, Frankfurt
- Ostello Bello, Genova
- Oasis Backpackers, Granada
- Balmers Hostel, Interlaken
- Rising Cock, Lagos
- Five Elements, Leipzig
- Celica Hostel, Ljubljana
- The People Hostel, Lille
- Sunset Destination, Lisbon
- St. Christophers, London
- Five Elements Hostel, Leipzig
- Cats Hostel, Madrid
- Vertigo Vieux Point, Marseille
- Ostello Bello, Milan
- Euro Youth Hotel, Munich
- Ostello Bello, Naples
- Villa Saint Exupery, Nice
- St. Christophers Inn Canal, Paris
- Cats Hostel, Porto
- Czech Inn, Prague
- Sunflower Hostel, Rimini
- Ostello Bello, Rome
- ROOM, Rotterdam
- Yoho, Salzburg
- City Backpackers, Stockholm
- Purple Nest, Valencia
- Anda Hostel, Venice
- St. Christopher's Hostel, Vienna
- OkiDoki, Warsaw

Know before you go

Where did it originate from?

The EU designated 2021 as the European Year of Rail, with the goal of establishing a new future for European passengers, encouraging greener options, and capitalizing on the old continent's extensive rail history.

The European Travel Commission and Eurail encouraged Famous Hostels to come up with creative strategies to stimulate train travel.

That's when we developed Eco-Wanderer, a platform for developing sustainable advertisements based on train travel. To initiate a debate about sustainable tourism, create awareness about sustainable travel, promote our local tourist companies, and have a direct influence on carbon emissions caused by travel. The goal is to reduce CO2 emissions by 3 billion kg throughout the campaign's 11 active months.

Contact

Email: info@FamousHostels.com

Website: www.famoushostels.com/eco-wanderer

French hub stations

France has many hub stations in Paris, including:

- Lyon
- Nord
- Austerlitz
- Bercy
- Est
- Montparnasse

From these rail stations, you may connect to trains to most of France's major cities.

Station Facilities

The major rail stations in France generally offer good amenities, which frequently include:

- Luggage lockers
- Foreign exchange desks
- Restaurants and cafés
- Tourist information offices
- ATM cash machines
- Elevators and escalators
- Access for travelers with disabilities.

Germany

Germany has plenty of attractive places, such as the lively capital Berlin, the picturesque Neuschwanstein Castle, and significant towns such as Cologne, Hamburg, and Munich. You may also explore the deep forest, mountainous regions, river valleys, and sea coast. In a nutshell, Germany has everything.

Routes Map

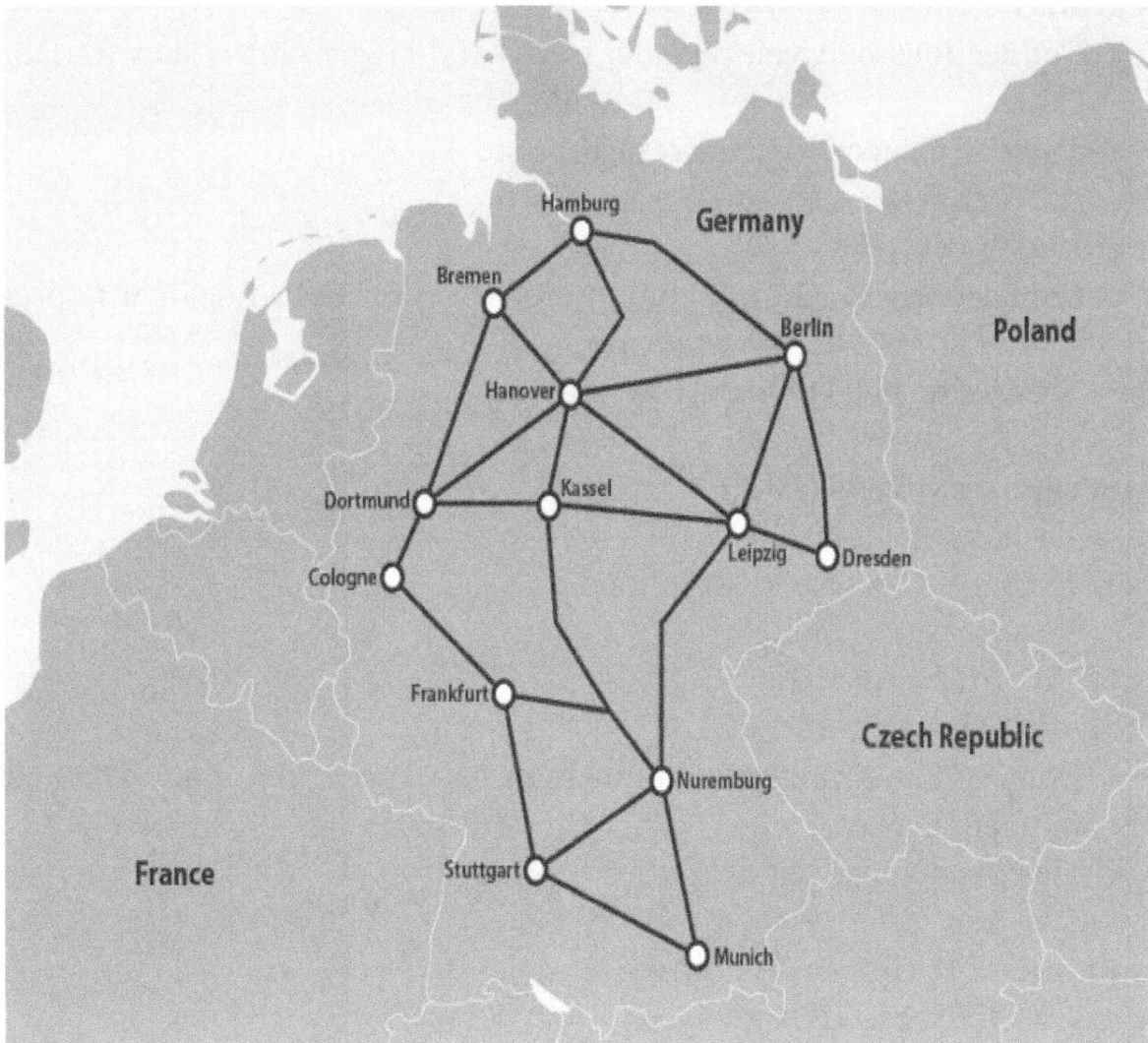

German train types

Domestic Train

Your Eurail Pass is also valid on various German train operators.

Regional and intercity trains in Germany
S-Bahn

- Suburban trains operate in most major cities.
- There is no need to make reservations.

Regional Express (RE)

- Connections between regional towns and bigger cities. They frequent stops.
- There is no need to make reservations.

Regional Bahn (RB)

- Connections to all local communities. Slower than Regional Express trains.
- There is no need to make reservations.

Interregio-Express (IRE)

links Germany's regions.
There is no need to make reservations.

InterCity and Eurocity
(Express) (IC, EC, and ECE)

- Domestic and international linkages between major cities. There are frequent pauses.
- There is no need to make reservations.

High-speed trains in Germany
InterCity Express (ICE)

- Connects major cities at speeds of up to 320 km/h (200 mph).
- There is a restaurant on board.

- First-class passengers may get additional privileges such as newspapers and power sockets.
- Reservations are unnecessary (but suggested during peak months).

TGV

- Frankfurt/Munich/Stuttgart/Freiburg to France.
- For journeys inside Germany, reservations are not required.
- Reservations are necessary for visits to France.

International trains

International high-speed trains in Germany

ICE

- Frankfurt - Paris/Brussels/Amsterdam/Zurich
- Stuttgart - Paris.
- Hamburg - Zurich
- Dortmund - Vienna
- Reservations for Frankfurt-Amsterdam are required during the summer season (June 17th to August 18th).
- All year, reservations for Frankfurt-Paris are required.

TGV

- Frankfurt - Paris - Marseille
- Munich/Stuttgart/Freiburg - Paris
- Frankfurt to Bordeaux. Saturdays, July 8 - August 26 Freiburg - Bordeaux. Saturdays, 01 April - 02 September
- For journeys inside Germany, reservations are not required.
- Reservations are necessary for visits to France.

Eurostar

- Dortmund - Düsseldorf - Cologne -
- Brussels - Paris
- Reservations must be made.
- former Thalys trains in red

- RailJet Munich - Salzburg/Vienna/Budapest
- When visiting Hungary, reservations are typically optional but required.

International conventional trains in Germany
EuroCity Express (ECE)

- Munich - Zurich
- Frankfurt - Milan

EuroCity (EC)

- Hamburg - Zurich/Interlaken
- Bochum - Klagenfurt
- Hamburg/Berlin - Prague - Budapest
- Berlin - Gdynia - Warsaw
- Berlin - Wroclaw - Krakow - Przemysl
- Frankfurt - Munich - Salzburg -
- Ljubljana - Zagreb
- Reservations are optional.
- Munich to Venice, Verona, and Bologna (Italy)
- If you are traveling to/from/within Italy, you must pay supplements. You may buy it before boarding, but you can also do it on the train (for a €5 cost).
  - First class: €15
  - €10 for 2nd class

InterCity (IC)

- Hamburg - Copenhagen/Aarhus
- Berlin - Amsterdam
- Hamburg - Zurich (NightJet)
- Amsterdam - Cologne - Frankfurt - Zurich (NightJet)
- Stuttgart - Zurich

Bordering nations' train stations

With a Eurail pass valid in Germany, you may travel to the following train stations in neighboring countries:

- Basel (Switzerland)
- Salzburg (Austria)

Night Trains

Domestic Night trains in Germany

ÖBB Nightjet (these trains continue or begin in other countries)

- Düsseldorf - Cologne - Frankfurt - Nürnberg - Munich
- Düsseldorf - Cologne - Frankfurt - Nürnberg - Passau
- Hamburg - Hannover - Frankfurt - Freiburg - Basel
- Berlin - Leipzig - Frankfurt - Freiburg - Basel
- Dresden - Leipzig - Frankfurt - Freiburg - Basel

International Night trains in Germany
Snälltget Night Train

Berlin - Hamburg - Copenhagen restad - Malmö - Stockholm

SJ Euronight (EN)
- Berlin (from 31 March) - Hamburg - Copenhagen Airport - Malmö - Stockholm

ÖBB NightJet (NJ and EN)
- Munich - Florence - Rome (not between 10 June and 9 September)
- Munich - Bologna - Ancona (10 June - 9 September)

- Munich - Verona - Milano - Genoa - La Spezia
- Stuttgart - Munich - Udine - Venice
- Hamburg - Basel - Zürich
- Hamburg - Linz - Vienna
- Hamburg - Munich - Innsbruck
- Hamburg - Nuremberg - Vienna
- Amsterdam/Brussels - Düsseldorf - Linz - Vienna
- Amsterdam - Düsseldorf - Cologne - Innsbruck
- Amsterdam - Düsseldorf - Cologne - Basel - Zürich
- Paris - Munich - Vienna
- Berlin - Wroclaw - Bratislava - Budapest
- Berlin - Wroclaw - Vienna - Graz
- Prague/Berlin - Leipzig - Basel - Zürich

EuroNight Imre Kálmán (EN)
- Stuttgart - Munich - Salzburg -
- Vienna - Budapest

EuroNight Lisinski (EN)
- Stuttgart - Munich - Ljubljana - Zagreb

EuroNight Opatija (EN)
- Stuttgart – Munich – Opatija – Rijeka

European Sleeper (ESL)
- Berlin - Amsterdam - Rotterdam - Den Haag - Antwerp - Brussels

Scenic Train
Scenic rail routes in Germany
Black Forest Line
From Offenburg to Konstanz, via the Black Forest and small communities.

Rhine Valley Line
Runs from Koblenz to Mainz, passing through the German wine area.

Elbe Valley Line
Runs from Dresden to Czechia along the Elbe River in Saxon Switzerland.

Neckar Valley Line
Connects Stuttgart and Heidelberg along the scenic Neckar River.

Mosel Valley Line
Runs from Koblenz to Trier, small towns, and wine along the Mosel River.

Domestic Routes
Seat reservations on ICE trains are not required in Germany. However, I urge that you get a seat reservation, particularly if you're going in a group. You will not be asked to leave your seat if you do not have a reservation.
View estimated train journey times between Germany's major cities with High-speed ICE trains.

Route	ICE
Berlin to Cologne	4h 30m
Berlin to Frankfurt	4h
Berlin to Hamburg	2h
Berlin to Munich	4h 30m

Frankfurt to Cologne	1h
Frankfurt to Munich	3h 30m
Hamburg to Cologne	4h
Hamburg to Frankfurt	4h
Hamburg to Munich	6h
Munich to Cologne	4h 30m

International Routes

Route	Which train?	Travel time	Reservations
Berlin to Amsterdam (Netherlands)	InterCity	6h 20m	Optional
Berlin to Prague (Czechia)	EuroCity	4h 30m	Optional

Berlin to Warsaw (Poland)	Berlin-Warsaw Express	5h 30m	Required
Berlin to Zurich (Switzerland)	ÖBB Nightjet	12h 15m (overnight)	Required
Dresden to Wroclaw (Poland)	*trilex* regional train	4h	Not required
Düsseldorf / Frankfurt to Amsterdam (Netherlands)	ICE	2h 15m / 3h 55m	Optional (Required June 17th till August 18th)
Frankfurt to Brussels (Belgium)	ICE	3h 05m	Optional
Frankfurt to Paris (France)	TGV / ICE	3h 55m	Required
Hamburg to Zurich (Switzerland)	ICE / ÖBB Nightjet	7h 35m / 10h 55m (overnight)	Optional / Required
Hamburg to Aarhus (Denmark)	IC train	4h 26m	Required from June 17th until August 21st

Hamburg to Copenhagen (Denmark)	IC train	4h 40m	Required from June 17th until August 21st
Munich to Innsbruck (Austria)	EuroCityBrenner	1h 45m	Recommended, supplement required
Munich to Paris (France)	<u>TGV</u>	5h 40m	Required
Munich to Rome (Italy)	<u>ÖBB Nightjet</u>	11h 30m (overnight)	Required
Munich to Venice (Italy)	EuroCityBrenner / <u>ÖBB Nightjet</u>	6h 50m / 8h 40m (overnight)	Recommended / Required
Munich to Vienna (Austria)	<u>RailJet</u>	4h 10m	Optional
Stuttgart to Zagreb (Croatia)	EuroCity / EuroNight	10h 45m / 14h 10m (overnight)	Required
Stuttgart to Budapest (Hungary)	EuroNight	12h 50m (overnight)	Required

Berlin – Stockholm	EuroNight / Snälltåget	15h 20m / 17h 15m (overnight)	Required
Berlin – Budapest (Hungary)	EuroCity / EuroNight	11h 30m / 13h 30m (overnight)	Required
Frankfurt – Milan (Italy)	EuroCity Express	7h 45m	Recommended
Berlin to Brussels (Belgium) via Amsterdam (Netherlands)	European Sleeper	11h 30m (overnight)	Required
Dortmund / Cologne to Paris (France)	Eurostar	5h 10m / 3h 20m	Required

Ferry Routes

International ferry links to and from Germany

You may also travel to and from Germany via ferry. With a Eurail pass, you may save money on specified routes.

- Finland - Germany
  Travemünde to Helsinki (Finland) or Sail with Finnlines from Rostock. Eurail passes provide a 30% savings.
- Poland - Germany

Travel from Rostock to Gdynia with Finnlines and save 30% with Eurail passes.

- Sweden - Germany
  Finnlines provides service from Travemünde to Malmö (Sweden). Eurail passes are 20% off.

Reservations

Reservation system for Eurail
- Eurail, IC, EC, ECE, ICE, TGV, RailJet,
- Eurostar, Nightjet, EuroNight

Booking via Eurail self-service costs administrative fees.
- EUR 2,- per person per train
- Additional € 9,- per order
  (for paper tickets)

With railway carriers
- DB (German Railways): Domestic and foreign trains
  - IC, EC, ICE, RailJet

- ÖBB (Austrian railways): Domestic and international trains
  - RailJet, IC, EC, ICE, Nightjet, EuroNight

- CD (Czech railways): Domestic and international trains
  - RailJet, IC, EC, ICE, Nightjet, EuroNight

- DSB (via b-europe): Domestic and international trains
  - IC, EC, ICE, RailJet

- Westbahn (Private Railway): Only international Westbahn trains are available.

- SNCB (b-europe): Only Eurostar trains.
- Snälltaget: Only the Berlin-Stockholm night train
- SJ (Swedish Railways): Only Berlin - Stockholm. Euro Night
- European Sleeper: Only European Sleeper trains, international

Calling Deutsche Bahn
- There are phone lines for English, French, Danish, Italian, Dutch, and German-speaking customer support representatives.

Locally in Germany, at the rail station
- Domestic only - At the DB ticket machines at the station

Good To Know
Which trains in Germany need reservations?
- No reservations: Regional (RE, RB, IR).
- Optional (but preferred during peak periods): InterCity (IC) / ICE / EuroCity (EC) / ECE (Eurocity Express). €4,50 for 2nd class and €5,90 for 1st class.
- All night trains are required; costs vary depending on the destination and the kind of seat/bed reserved.
- ICE trains from and to Amsterdam are required during the summer season (€4,50 from 17 June to 18 August).
- In the summer season, IC trains from and to Denmark are required (€4,50 from 17 June to 21 August).
- Supplement Eurocity (EC) trains to/from/within Italy. Optional for routes that do not begin, terminate, or go through Italy.

The ICE Paris-Frankfurt train has a limited number of seats available for Eurail Pass holders. My advice is to book this train well in advance, particularly if you want to travel during peak season (May to September).

Eurostar trains are popular and, as a result, frequently sell out rapidly. Make sure you obtain your seat reservation in advance. Alternatively, you may select trains without seat reservations in our schedule by clicking the 'no reservation required' option.

German Rail Pass

- Eurail One Country Pass is not available in Germany .
- If you simply want to travel in Germany, look into the German Rail Pass.
- Prices start at $ 167

Global Pass.

- Feel free to tour Germany and the other 32 European countries.
- Standard pricing begins at $ 211.

Germany Tips and Techniques

Quick Facts
Capital: Berlin
Population: 81.1 million
Language: German
Currency: Euro (EUR)
Dialing code: +49

The spelling of city names

On German rail timetables and at German train stations, you'll normally discover the local spelling of German towns and stations.
Here is the local spelling of several well-known German cities:

- Hanover = Hannover
- Cologne = Köln
- Munich = München
- Nürnberg = Nürnberg

German Hub Stations

The major hub stations in Germany are Berlin Hbf, Köln Hbf (Cologne), München Hbf (Munich), and Frankfurt Hbf. Trains to Germany's major cities and numerous overseas locations may be boarded at these rail stations.

Station facilities

Stations in Germany often offer good amenities, which frequently include:
- Luggage storage
- Foreign exchange desks
- Restaurants and cafés
- Tourist information offices
- ATM cash machines
- Elevators and escalators
- Access for travelers with disabilities

Get around with the S-Bahn

Eurail Pass users may ride for free on DB's S-Bahn (suburban metro train) networks in key German cities. The S-Bahn is distinguished by its logo (a white S on a green backdrop).

Ferry busses to and from Germany

The German Rail Pass includes free bus travel (reservations required). Travel from Germany to France, Switzerland, the Netherlands to italy, and many more countries

.

Other advantages
- Check out for European famous hostels in France guide, the same applies.

Italy

Traveling by rail in Italy allows you to see everything, from the ancient relics of Pompeii to the stunning Tuscan coastline. Explore the various wonders of Rome and Florence, go shopping in Milan, and boat across the canals of Venice. The whole country is within your reach with a Eurail Pass and pleasant Italian trains!

Route Map

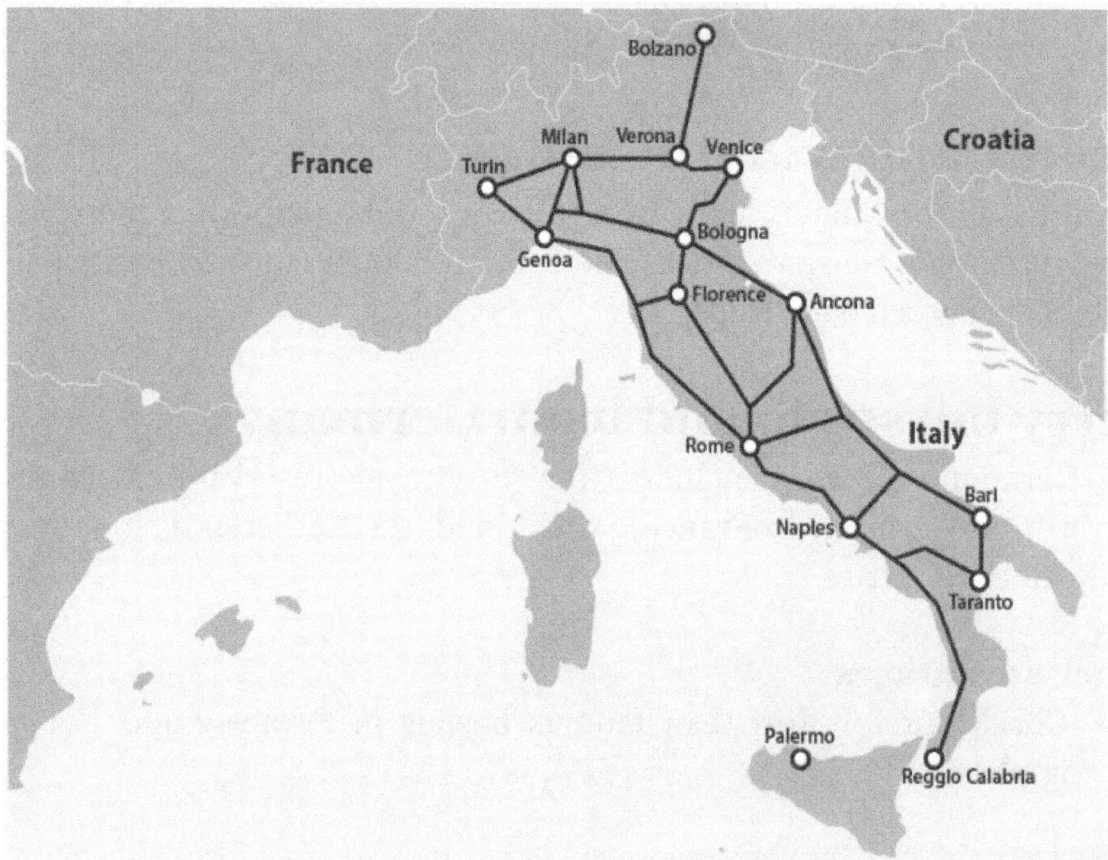

Italy Train type

Domestic Trains
Regional and intercity trains

Trenord regionale (R)

- runs across the central northern region of Lombardia, near Switzerland.
- There is no need to make reservations.
- Trains between Lecco and Piona are not covered in your Pass.
- Milan and Malpensa airport trains are not included in your Pass.
- Train schedules for Trenitalia can be found at www.viaggiatreno.it/infomobilita/index.jsp.

InterCity (IC)

- Connects major cities such as Florence, Milan, Rome, and Venice.
- Faster than regional trains and with fewer stops.
- Reservations must be made.

The Leonardo Express

- A rapid train that connects Rome with Fiumicino Airport.
- Because all seats are first class, a first-class Eurail Pass is necessary to ride on this train. If you have a 2nd Class Eurail Pass, you will need to purchase a ticket.
- Passholders in the second class may use Frecciarossa trains between Rome and Fiumicino airport.

Domestic high-speed trains

The Le Frecce high-speed trains (previously Eurostar Italia) are contemporary and pleasant. All trains offer air conditioning, luggage racks, power sockets, snacks, and, in most cases, a restaurant car.

Frecciarossa (FR)

- is a high-speed rail network that connects the major Italian cities from north to south.
- The fastest trains in Italy, reaching speeds of up to 300 km/h.
- The Frecciarossa 1000 is the flagship model.
- Reservations are necessary.

Fiumicino Airport (Rome) to and from Frecciarossa (FR)
- Fiumicino - Roma Termini
- Fiumicino - Napoli (via Roma Termini)
- Fiumicino - Venezia S. Lucia (via Bologna, Florence, Roma Termini)
- Reservations are necessary.

Frecciargento (FA)
- Connects the major Italian cities from north to south via high-speed and regular railway lines.
- With speeds of up to 250 km/h, it is Italy's second-fastest train.
- Reservations are necessary.

Frecciabianca (FB)
- Connects major Italian cities with secondary ones via traditional railway lines.
- With speeds of up to 200 km/h, it is Italy's third-fastest train.
- Reservations are necessary.

Freccialink (Frecce + bus)
- Trenitalia provides bus connections via Freccialink to communities that are otherwise inaccessible by rail.
- However, Freccialink bus bookings may only be made at train stations in Italy and by phone. @ www.trenitalia.com/it/informazioni/i_nostri_call_center.html
- They can only be booked in conjunction with Le Frecce trains. @ www.trenitalia.com/it/le_frecce/servizio_freccialink.html

International trains
- EuroCity Brenner connects Venice, Verona, and Bologna to Munich, Germany, via Innsbruck, Austria.
- Reservations are optional.
- If you are going to/from/within Italy, there is a mandatory supplement.

- First class: €15
- €10 for 2nd class
- A supplement of €5 can be purchased on board.

EuroCity to Switzerland
- Connects Milan and Venice to Zurich, Bern, Basel, and Geneva (Switzerland).
- Reservations must be made.

EuroCity (Express)
- Connects Milan to Frankfurt (Germany) via Basel (Switzerland).
- Reservations are required if you are going to/from/within Italy.

EuroCity to Austria via Slovenia
- Connects Vienna via Graz (Austria) and Trieste to Ljubljana (Slovenia)
- Reservations are optional.

Railjet
- Connects Venice/Bolzano to Vienna (Austria).
- Seat reservations are optional.
- If you are going to/from/within Italy, this is a required addition.
  - First class: €15
  - €10 for 2nd class
  - A supplement may be purchased on board for €5

TGV
- Connects Turin/Milan to several French cities.
- Reservations must be made.

Intercity and Regional Trains to Nice
- Connects Milan and Genoa to Nice and the Côte d'Azur (France).
- Step 1: IC Milan - RE Genoa - Ventimiglia / Genoa - Ventimiglia
- Step 2: RE Ventimiglia - Monaco - Nice - Cannes (France)

- Transfer to Ventimiglia

Night Trains

Domestic Night Trains:

Travel between the north and south of Italy at night, saving you valuable travel time as you sleep. These are the domestic night trains that run in Italy:

InterCity Notte (ICN) to Sicily

This is a one-of-a-kind adventure since the train is carried by boat across the Strait of Messina.

- Milan - Bologna - Firenze - Messina - Catania - Syracusa
- Milan - Bologna - Firenze - Messina - Palermo
- Rome - Napoli - Salerno - Messina - Catania - Syracusa
- Rome - Napoli - Salerno - Messina - Palermo
- Rome - Messina - Catania - Syracusa
- Rome - Messina - Palermo

InterCity Notte (ICN)

between the rest of Italy

- Milan - Bari - Taranto - Brinsidi - Lecce
- Milan - Parma - Bari - Brinsidi - Lecce
- Torino - Alessandria - Bari - Brinsidi - Lecce
- Torino - Milan - Roma - Napoli - Salerno
- Torino - Genoa - Roma - Napoli - Salerno

- Torino - Genoa - Pisa -
  Livorno - Reggio di Calabria
- Trieste - Venice - Padova - Rome
- Bolzano - Trento - Verona - Rome

International Night Trains:
Night trains link Italy with Austria, Germany, and Spain, saving you time and money. These night trains go to and from Italy:

ÖBB Nightjet (EN) provides several trains that link to and from various Italian destinations:
- Rome - Florence - Salzburg - Munich (Not between 10 June and 9 September)
- Ancona - Bologna - Salzburg - Munich - Stuttgart (10 June - 9 September)
- Rome - Florence - Bologna - Vienna
- Ancona - Bologna - Vienna
  (10 June - 9 September)
- Livorno - Pisa - Florence - Bologna - Vienna (Not between 10 June and 9 September)
- La Spezia - Genoa - Milan -
  Verona - Vienna
- La Spezia - Genoa - Milan - Verona - Salzburg - Munich - Stuttgart
- Venice - Udine - Salzburg - Vienna
- Venice - Udine - Salzburg -
  Munich - Stuttgart
- Reservations for overnight accommodations are necessary.

Italy's Scenic Rail Routes
Two scenic train routes travel into Italy:

| Bernina Express | Chur – Lugano (Switzerland) via Tirano (Italy |

| Centovalli Railway | Locarno (Switzerland) – Domodossola (Italy) |

Domestic Routes

Italy boasts an extensive high-speed rail network that will get you where you want to go much quicker than the regional train system. However, on high-speed trains, you must make a seat reservation.

How long does it take to go by rail between Italy's major cities? Check out the estimated timings for both regional and high-speed Italian trains:

Route	Regional	High-speed
Rome to Florence	3h 30m	1h 30m
Rome to Milan	9h (1 stop)	3h
Rome to Venice	9h (3 stops)	3h 30m
Florence to Milan	5h 30m (1 stop)	1h 30m
Florence to Venice	4h (2 stops)	2h
Pisa to Florence	1h	1h
Venice to Milan	3h 30m (1 stop)	2h 30m

Milan to Naples	14h	4h 35m
Rome to Turin	10h 20m	4h 10m
Milan to Palermo	-	20h 45m (overnight)

International routes

Route	Which train?	Travel time	Reservations
Genova (via Ventimiglia) to Nice (France)	IC + Regional trains	3h 15m	Required
Milan to Bern / Geneva / Zurich (Switzerland)	EuroCity	3h / 4h 15m / 3h 15m	Required
Milan to Vienna (Austria)	ÖBB Nightjet	11h 30m (overnight)	Required
Rome to Munich (German)	EuroCity Brenner / ÖBB Nightjet	6h 20m / 13h (overnight)	Required

Venice to Innsbruck (Austria)	EuroCity Brenner	4h 30m	Required
Venice to Vienna (Austria)	RailJet	8h (overnight)	Required
Venice to Vienna (Austria)	EuroNight	7h 30m (overnight)	Required
Trieste to Ljubljana (Slovenia)	EuroCity	3h	Optional

Ferry Routes
Spain-Italy

Grimaldi Lines offers ferry service from Barcelona, Spain, to Civitavecchia and Porto Torres (Sardinia), Italy. Eurail Italy Pass holders get a 20% discount.

Grimaldi Lines ferry

Grimaldi Lines provides a choice of routes to Greece, Spain, Italy, and its stunning island of Sardinia. Admire Europe's stunning coastlines while relaxing on the decks of Grimaldi Lines' boats. Dive into a world of entertainment and luxury with a variety of onboard services. Choose this swift and pleasant boat voyage to cut lengthy treks between countries.

Grimaldi Lines routes

The most essential routes are as follows:

- Barcelona (Spain) - Civitavecchia (Italy)
  via Porto Torres (Sardinia)
- Barcelona (Spain) - Savona (Italy)
- Civitavecchia (Italy) - Porto Torres (Sardinia)
- Brindisi (Italy) - Igoumenitsa (Greece)
- Brindisi (Italy) - Patras (Greece)
- Livorno (Italy) - Palermo (Italy)
- Livorno (Italy) - Olbia (Italy)
- Salerno (Italy) - Palermo (Italy)
- Salerno (Italy) - Catania (Italy)

Services and Facilities
- Bar Café Casino
- Children's play area
- Cinema
- Disabled facilities
- Disco
- Live onstage entertainment
- Sockets for power
- Restaurant/bistro
- Shops
- Swimming pool
- Displays for video
- WiFi internet

Facilities vary depending on the ferry and route.

Additional information

Discounts for Eurail Pass holders
Eurail Pass users get a 20% discount on ship travel and a 10% discount on lodging (cabin, berth, or Pullman seats).
Port taxes, fixed dues, fuel surcharges, and prices for on-board services and meals are not included in the discount.

How to reserve

- Online at www.grimaldi-lines.com by choosing the agreement EURAIL PASS from the Partnership list and entering your Pass Cover code in the relevant form. You can locate your Pass Cover code in your Travel Diary, which is circled in the figure below.
- Please keep in mind that if you are traveling with a mobile Pass, you must contact customer service to get a Pass Cover number before making a reservation with Grimaldi Lines.

- By phone, dial (+39) 081 496 444 (Italy) or (+34) 902 531 333 (Spain).

- Contact info@grimaldi.napoli.it or reservas@grimalditour.com via email. Please keep in mind that if you make your bookings by email, you must give Grimaldi Lines a copy of your Eurail Pass.

- you can make your reservation at a Grimaldi Lines Travel Agency in Italy:
    - Grimaldi Tours Napoli, Via Marchese Campodisola 13,
    - Grimaldi Tours Roma, Via Boncompagni 43
    - Grimaldi Tours Palermo, Via Emerico Amari 8,

- or the Grimaldi Lines Port Offices in Civitavecchia, Livorno, or Barcelona.
- Always provide your Eurail Pass Cover number.

Your discount will be applied when you book your reservation.

Greece-Italy

- Patras in Greece to Ancona on Italy's Adriatic coast or Sail with Minoan Lines from Igoumenitsa. With a Eurail Italy Pass, you may travel for free or at a reduced cost.

Minoan Lines Ferry Discounts

Minoan Lines provides ferry service inside Greece as well as between Greece and Italy. If you have a pass that is valid in both Italy and Greece, you may enjoy cheap deck passage. Onboard, you may make use of the various facilities, such as swimming in the pool or going to the cinema.
Ferry route:

- Venice (Italy) - Patras (Greece)
- Venice (Italy) - Igoumenitsa (Greece)
- Ancona (Italy) - Patras (Greece)
  via Igoumenitsa
- Ancona (Italy) - Igoumenitsa (Greece)
- Piraeus (Greece) - Heraklion (Crete)

Services and Facilities

- Casino bar
- Children's play area Cinema
- Disabled facilities
- Disco Restaurant/Bistro Shops
- Swimming pool
- Video screens

- WiFi internet

Facilities vary depending on the ferry and route.

Additional information

Discounts and terms for Eurail pass holders

On Greek internal and Adriatic routes (run by Grimaldi Lines):

If your Eurail Pass is valid in Italy or Greece, you may save 20% off deck passage rates as well as 20% off all passenger accommodation categories. You may get your discount by displaying your Pass before purchasing your ticket.

This deal is valid for both 1st and 2nd class Eurail card holders. A fuel fee may apply.

Check-in is two hours before departure.

Reservation and information

To make a reservation,

- Send an email to booking@minoan.gr or
- call +30 210 414 5700 in Greece or
- +39 041 240 7177 in Italy.

Reservations

Eurail reservation self-service system

- Eurail, IC, EC, Frecce (domestic),
- TGV, RailJet, Nightjet

Booking via Eurail self-service costs administrative fees.

- EUR 2,- per person per train
- Additional € 9,- per order
  (for paper tickets)

With railway carriers
- ÖBB (Austrian Railways): Domestic and foreign trains

Other online services
- Italiarail

Locally in Italy, at the rail station

By Phone
Reservations may be made by calling the Trenitalia call center (www.trenitalia.com/en/services/our_call_centres.html).

Good to know
Which trains in Italy need reservations?
- No reservations: Regional trains operated by Trenitalia.
- Frecciarossa, Frecciagento, Frecciabianca, Intercity, and Intercity are all required. Notte trains

Reservations for the TGV (Paris-Milan)
- Seats are restricted for Eurail Pass holders.
- Tickets and bookings for this route are not available at Italian rail stations.

Italy Pass

- Spend your whole trip visiting Italy by train.
- Standard pricing begins at $ 145.

Global Pass
- Feel free to tour Italy and the other 32 European countries.
- Standard pricing begins at $ 211.

Italy Travel Tips and Tricks

Quick Facts

- The capital is Rome.
- 60 million people
- Language: Italian
- Currency: Euro (EUR)
- Dialing code: +39

Italian cities on timetables

The local spelling of Italian towns and stations may typically be seen on rail timetables and at train stations.

Here is the local spelling of several well-known Italian cities:

- Florence = Firenze
- Genoa = Genova
- Milan = Milano
- Naples = Napoli
- Padua = Padova
- Pompeii = Pompei
- Rome = Roma
- Sicily (island) = Sicilia
- Turin = Torino
- Venice = Venezia

Italian Hub Stations

The two major hub stations in Italy are Roma Termini in Rome and Milano Centrale in Milan. From these rail stations, you may connect to trains to most of Italy's major cities.

Station Facilities

Stations in Italy often offer excellent facilities, which frequently include:

- Luggage lockers

- Foreign exchange desks
- Restaurants and cafés
- Tourist information offices
- ATM cash machines
- Elevators and escalators
- Access for travelers with disabilities.

Portugal

Traveling by rail in Portugal will take you to some of the most intriguing and varied sites conceivable. Discover the white sand beaches of the Algarve, the exquisite wines of Porto, and the magnificent energy of Lisbon with your Eurail pass. It's all yours to explore with your Eurail Portugal Pass!

Routes map

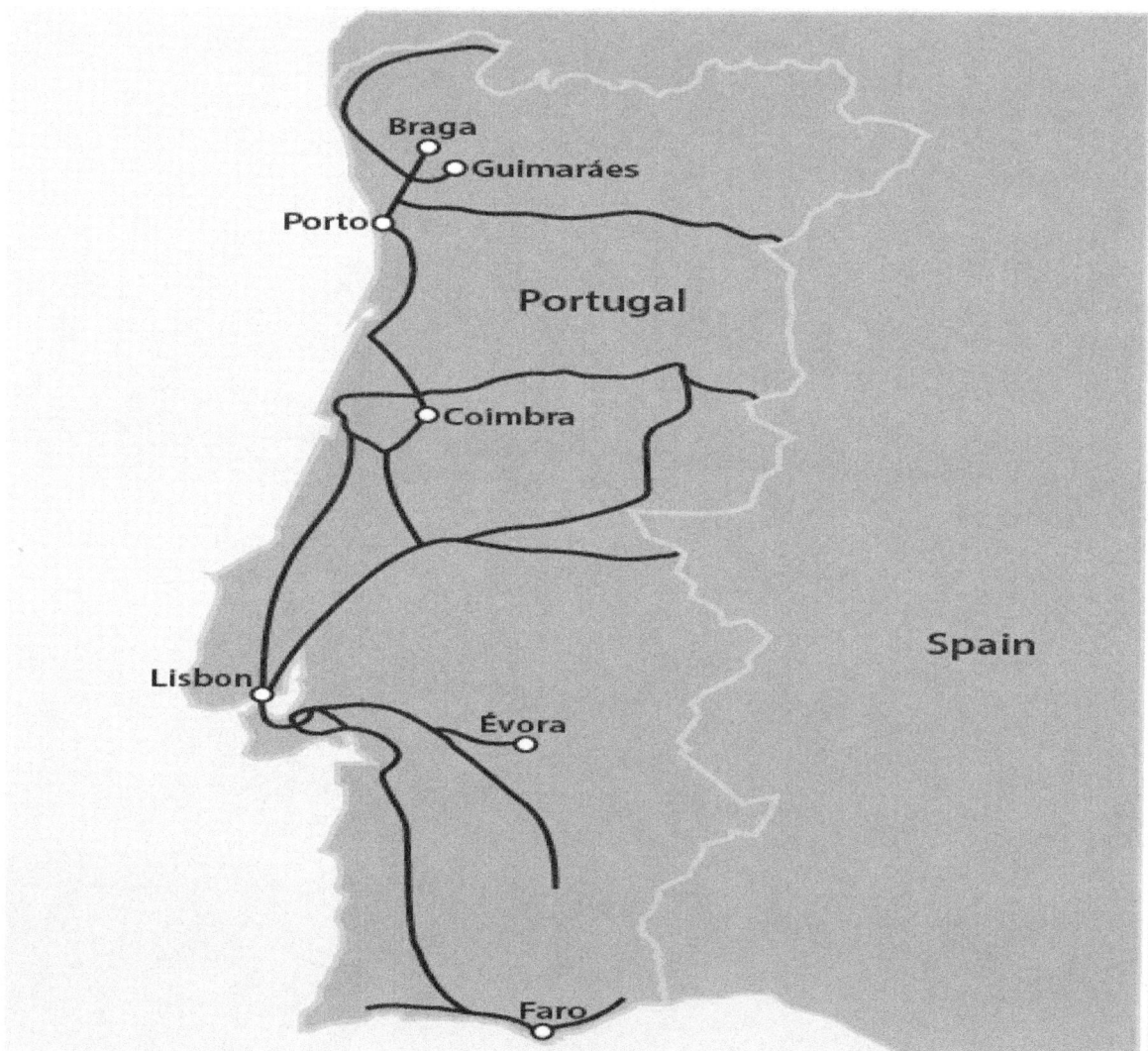

Train types

Domestic Train

There are several trains in Portugal that will take you around the nation at any time of day or night. CP (Comboios de Portugal) runs the Portuguese network.

Regional and Intercity Trains in Portugal
Regional (RE / TRN) and Inter-Regional (RE)

- Trains link bigger cities such as Lisbon and Porto to smaller towns. They make several stops over short distances.
- There is no need for a reservation

Intercity / Intercidades (IC)

- Faster trains linking large towns and cities, with fewer stops along the way.
- Reservations are necessary.

Urbanos (SUB)

- suburban commuter trains that run in and around Lisbon and Porto.
- There is no need for a reservation.
- You may take the following Urbanos lines:
  - Lisbon to Azambuja, Lisbon to Cascais, Lisbon to Sintra (a tourist favorite!) Lisbon to Sado Porto to Aveiro, Porto to Braga, Porto to Cade/Marco de Canaveses, and Porto to Guimares

High-speed trains in Portugal
Alfa Pendular (AP)

- Domestic high-speed rail linking Guimares, Braga, Porto, Coimbra, Lisbon, and Faro.
- Portugal's fastest train.
- A reservation is needed.

International Trains
International trains in Portugal

- Celta (INT) International train that connects Porto (Campanha) and Vigo (Guixar) in Spain.
- A Spanish railway collaboration between CP and RENFE.
- A reservation is necessary (there is no cost at the train station).

IC & Regional rail (RE)

- Lisbon/Porto - Madrid (Spain).
  - Connecting trains run from Lisbon/Porto to Entroncamento.
  - Entroncamento - Badajoz.
  - By IC, Badajoz to Madrid.
  - Reservations are needed for Lisbon/Porto - Entroncamento and Badajoz - Madrid.

Popular Connections
Domestic trains

Here are estimated train timings connecting Portugal's most popular cities by high-speed or regional trains. If you want to travel on a high-speed train, you must normally book your seat in advance.

You do not need to make reservations while using slower regional trains. You'll have to change trains on one or more times, which will add time to your travel.

Route	High-speed	Regional
Lisbon to Braga	3h 16m	7h 50m

Lisbon to Coimbra	1h 40m	3h 30m
Lisbon to Faro	3h 30m	-
Lisbon to Porto	2h 35m	6h 40m

International trains

I recommend the following routes to travel between Portugal and other European countries:

Route	Which train?	Duration	Reservations
Porto to Vigo (Spain)	Celta	2h 20m	Required
Lisbon to Madrid (Spain) via Badajoz	IC + RE + IC	9h	Required (Lisbon-Entroncamento & Badajoz-Madrid)
Porto to Madrid (Spain) via Badajoz	IC + RE + IC	11h	Required (Porto-Entroncamento & Badajoz-Madrid)

Porto to Madrid (Spain) via Vigo	IC + RE + ALV	11h	Required (Pontevedra-Madrid)

Reservations

How can I book rail tickets in Portugal?

- Local railway stations in Portugal. This is incredibly simple to do. Make them up to 60 days in advance at any of the CP Ticket Offices.
- Only at an international rail station can you reserve a seat on an international train.

If you want help, please contact CP at (+351) 707 210 220.

Portugal Pass

- Spend your whole trip visiting Portugal by train.
- Standard pricing starts at $ 92.

Global Pass

- Have the flexibility to visit Portugal and up to 32 other European countries.
- Standard pricing begins at $ 211.

Portugal Tips and Techniques

Quick facts

- Lisbon (Lisboa in Portuguese) is the capital.
- Population: 10.5 million
- Language: Portuguese
- Currency: Euro (EUR)
- +351: dialing code.

Portuguese hub stations

Portugal's major hub stations are Santa Apolónia in Lisbon and Campanha in Porto. Trains to Portugal's major cities and overseas destinations may be connected at these rail stops.

Station Facilities

- Stations in Portugal often offer good amenities, which frequently include:
- Luggage storage
- Foreign exchange desks
- Restaurants and cafés
- ATM cash machines in tourist information offices
- Elevators and escalators
- Access for travelers with disabilities

Greece

Your Eurail adventure through Greece will most likely be memorable. Greece is a mysterious combination of ancient history and modern-day hedonism. Take in the vistas that transport you to a world before time, and then return to the present for some sand, sea, and sun relaxation. Greece is a wonderful paradise, whether on the mainland or one of the many islands.

Because of operational concerns, Greece is presently not linked by train to other nations. It is, nevertheless, feasible to board a ferry from Italy to Greece.

Hellenic Train, a Greek railway company, runs services between several of the country's major cities, including Athens and Thessaloniki.

Routes Map

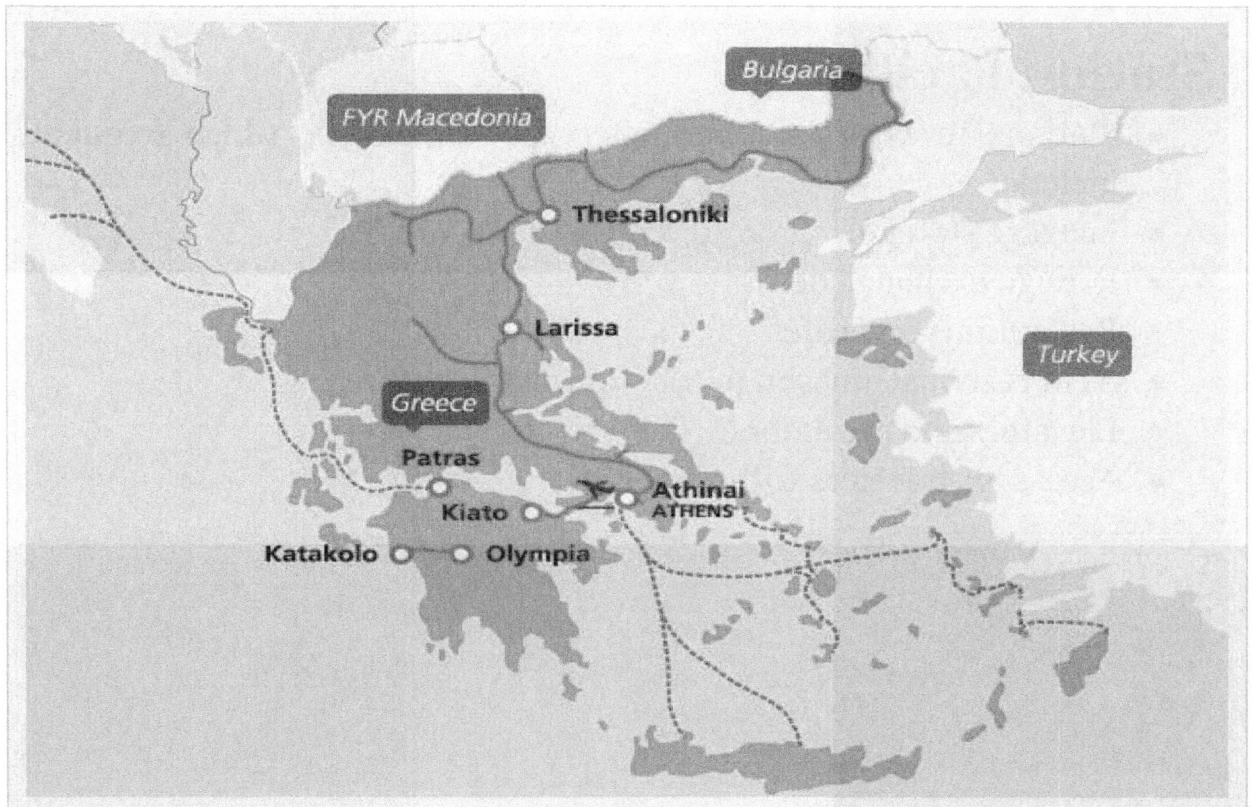

Train types in Greece

Domestic trains in Greece

Eurail Pass users can travel on all Hellenic trains. Eurail passengers simply have to pay the InterCity (IC) train supplements and any extra levies.

InterCity

- Athens - Larissa - Thessaloniki
- Larissa - Thessaloniki
- Larissa - Volos
- Athens - Kalambaka
- Reservations are necessary (but are free of charge).

Suburban railway

- Connects large urban areas to the suburbs.
- Available in Athens, Thessaloniki, and Patras.
- Reservations are not necessary.

Bicycles are permitted as check-in luggage on certain trains. Please check with the train stations to see if any fees apply.

International Trains

There is now no international rail travel from Thessaloniki to North Macedonia, Bulgaria, or Turkey. When their services will restart is presently unknown.

Popular connections
Domestic routes

Route	InterCity travel times
Athens to Thessaloniki	4h 40m
Athens to Larissa	3h
Larissa to Thessaloniki	1h 35m
Athens to Patras (Partially by bus)	2h 55m
Athens to Kalambaka	4h 21m

Greece's scenic rail routes
The Pelion train

- A steam train runs up Mount Pelion from Ano Lehonia to Miles.
- The trip takes 1.5 hours, including a 15-minute break.

The Rack Railway

- A rack railway runs from Diakofto to Kalavryta, passing through the breathtaking Vouraikos Gorge.
- The trip takes around one hour.

International ferry routes from Greece to Italy

Eurail Pass users with a Pass valid in both Greece and Italy obtain FREE and reduced ferry travel to Italy on the following routes:

Superfast Ferries

- Patras/Igoumenitsa to Ancona/Bari/Venice
- Corfu - Bari (summer only)

Reservations

- It is not possible to make a reservation using the Eurail reservation self-service system.
- locally at the train station

Greece Pass

- Spend your whole trip traveling by train around Greece.
- Prices start at $ 92 for the

Global Pass

- Explore Greece and up to 30 more countries by rail.
- Standard pricing begins at $ 211.

Greek Islands Pass

- Travel via ferry between Greece and Italy while go island hopping in Greece.
- Prices start at $77.

Greece Travel Tips and Tricks

Quick facts

- Athens is the capital
- Population is 10.8 million people.
- Language: Greek
- Euro (EUR)
- Dialing code: +30

The spelling of city names

On Greek rail timetables and at Greek train stations, you'll normally discover the local spelling of Greek towns and stations. Here is the local spelling of several well-known Greek cities:

- Athens = Athina
- Corfu = Kérkyra
- Corinth = Kórinthos
- Heraklion = Iráklio
- Patras = Pátra
- Piraeus = Pireàs

Ferry crossings between Greece and Italy

If your Eurail pass is valid in both Greece and Italy, you may travel for free with a variety of ferry providers. Those who only have Eurail passes for one of these countries may save up to 30% on full prices on specified trips.

Domestic Ferry Tips

The following ferry operators provide discounted domestic boat travel:

- Blue Star Ferries
- Superfast Ferries
- Minoan Lines

Greece Eurail aid offices.

If you have any queries concerning Eurail, you may contact the Hellenic Railways travel agency in Athens, the Patras train station, or the Thessaloniki Central train Station.

Detailed information about Eurail help offices in Greece.
Greece
- Athens Central Station: international ticketing window
- Monday through Friday: 8:00 a.m. to 4:00 p.m.

Links to airports

There is an hourly train from Athens E.Venizelos airport to Athens Central Railway Station and Kiato New Railway Station (change at Ano Liossia station).

Austria

The greatest way to see Austria is by train. Incredible natural beauty, exquisite towns like Vienna and Salzburg, and centuries of history are all waiting to be found. Travel across the Alps with your Eurail Pass to discover all of the riches that await you in this amazing nation.

Routes Map

Train types in Austria

In Austria, you can travel by rail at any time of day or night. The majority of the Austrian network is operated by BB (sterreichische Bundesbahnen).

Domestic trains

Regional and intercity trains in Austria

REX

- Commuter trains link Vienna with cities around it.
- Train timetables are provided on the OBB route planner.

S-Bahn

- A suburban metro rail network that operates inside Austria's largest cities.
- Journeys on the S-Bahn in Vienna, Salzburg (excluding lines S1 and S11), and Innsbruck are free with an Interrail Pass.

InterCity (IC)

- trains link bigger cities in Austria, such as Vienna, Innsbruck, Salzburg, and Graz.
- Reservations are unnecessary but suggested during peak season (May to September) and on public holidays.

Intercity bus (ICB)

- This bus travels between Graz and Klagenfurt.
- Reservations are necessary.

EuroCity (EC)

- connects Innsbruck, Salzburg, Graz, and Kufstein.
- Reservations are unnecessary but suggested during peak season (May to September) and on public holidays.

Domestic high-speed trains

Railjet (RJ)

- connects Vienna to major Austrian cities such as Innsbruck, Salzburg, and Graz.
- Reservations are unnecessary but suggested during peak season (May to September) and on public holidays.

WESTBahn

- München (Germany) and WESTBahn connects Vienna to Linz, Salzburg, Innsbruck.
- Westbahn offers special upgrades to Passholders.

International Trains

International high-speed trains in Austria

Railjet

- Connects Austria with various European cities with the following routes:
- Vienna - Linz - Munich - Stuttgart - Frankfurt
- Vienna - Gyor - Budapest
- Graz - Vienna - Brno - Prague
- Bratislava - Vienna - Salzburg - Innsbruck - Zurich
- Vienna - Graz - Villach - Venice

RegioJet

- The yellow RegioJet trains link Vienna with Brno and Prague (Czech Republic). To ride on this train, you must have an Interrail Global Pass. RegioJet enables reservations.

ICE

The following roads connect Austria to various German cities:
- Vienna - Nürnberg - Frankfurt - Cologne - Dortmund
- Vienna - Nürnberg - Erfurt -
- Berlin - Hamburg

InterCity buses
- Run from Villach and Udine in Italy and Klagenfurt in Austria to Venice.

EuroCity
- Connects Austria to various European cities via the routes:
  - Vienna - Ljubljana - Trieste
  - Graz - Vienna - Ostrava - Krakow
    - Rzesów - Przemysl
  - Klagenfurt - Salzburg - Munich
    - Cologne - Dortmund
  - Zagreb - Ljubljana - Salzburg
    - Munich - Frankfurt

- Munich - Innsbruck - Verona - Venice/Bologna/Rimini
  - If you are traveling to/from/within Italy, you must pay a supplement.
  - First-class: €15
  - €10 for 2nd class
  - A supplement can be purchased on the train for an additional fee costing another €5

Night Trains in Austria
Night trains go from Austria to France, Slovenia, Croatia, Serbia, Poland, Germany, Italy, Hungary, the Netherlands, Czechia, and Switzerland:

ÖBB Nightjet (NJ):
- Vienna - Florence - Rome (not available from 12 June to 08 September)
- Vienna - Bologna - Ancona (from 12 June to 08 September)
- Vienna - Verona - Milan - Genoa - La Spezia

- Vienna - Linz - Udine - Venice
- Vienna - Linz - Zürich
- Vienna - Linz - Munich - Stuttgart - Paris
- Vienna - Nürnberg - Hannover - Hamburg
- Vienna - Nürnberg - Cologne - Düsseldorf - Amsterdam
- Innsbruck - Munich - Cologne - Düsseldorf - Amsterdam
- Innsbruck - Munich - Hannover - Hamburg
- Graz - Vienna - Wroclaw - Berlin
- Graz - Innsbruck - Zurich

EuroNight (EN)

- Graz - Vienna - Katowice - Krakow - Warsaw (EN Chopin)
- Bratislava - Vienna - Graz - Maribor - Split
- Stuttgart - Salzburg - Villach - Ljubljana - Zagreb/Rijeka (EN Lisinski)
- Stuttgart - Munich - Linz - Vienna - Budapest (EN Kalman Imre)
- Zurich - Feldkirch - Innsbruck - Vienna - Budapest (EN Kalman Imre)
- Zurich - Feldkirch - Innsbruck - Ljubljana - Zagreb (EN Alpine Pearls)
- Zurich - Feldkirch - Innsbruck - Ceske Budejovice - Prague

Private railway
Private railway enterprises in Austria

The following private railway operators accept Eurail Passes on their trains:

- Micotra trains travel between Villach and Tarvisio (Italy).
- WESTbahn trains link Vienna and Salzburg.

- WESTbahn offers 1st class ticket holders an upgrade to WESTbahn PLUS for just €9.90. With this, you can enjoy premium seats, a complimentary welcome gift, and a newspaper, as well as beverage services delivered to your seat. You can obtain this upgrade on the train.
- Raaberbahn, from Neusiedl/See to Pamhagen (Gr) and ONLY from Ebenfurt to Sopron. RegioJet, yellow trains that go to the Czech Republic. To ride on this train, you must have a Eurail Global Pass.

The following private railway companies do not accept Eurail Passes on its trains:

- Pinzgauer Lokalbahn, which runs between Krimml and Zell am See.
- NVOG (containing the Mariazellerbahn, Wachaubahn, Waldviertelbahn, Reblaus Express, Citybahn Waidhofen, and Schneebergbahn)
- BB Postbus Stubaitalbahn
- Wiener Lokalbahnen
- Pinzgauer Lokalbahn
- Graz-Köflacher Eisenbahn
- Montafonerbahn
- Salzburger Lokalbahn
  (only S1 and S11 trains do not accept Interrail)
- Steiermärkische Landesbahnen
- Stern and Hafferl
- Zillertalbahn
- Salzkammergutbahn
- Achenseebahn

Travel to Liechtenstein

Liechtenstein

Liechtenstein is a small nation located between Austria and Switzerland. If your Eurail pass is valid in Austria, you may also travel to Liechtenstein. From Feldkirch in Austria to Buchs in Switzerland, there is a ÕBB train link via Liechtenstein. Liechtenstein has four tiny rail stations: Forst Hilti, Schaan-Vaduz, Nendeln, and Schaanwald. It is a short bus trip from Schaan-Vaduz to Liechtenstein's capital Vaduz (the bus is not included in your Eurail ticket).

Popular Connection
Domestic Relations

View estimated train travel times between Austria's most popular cities utilizing high-speed trains that do not need reservations.

Route	Travel time
Graz to Salzburg	2h 30m
Innsbruck to Salzburg	1h 50m
Innsbruck to Vienna	4h 15m

Salzburg to Vienna	2h 30m
Salzburg to Villach	2h 30m
Vienna to Villach	4h 15m

International Connection

I recommend the following routes for travel between Austria and other European countries:

Route	Which train?	Travel time	Reservations
Vienna to Amsterdam / Brussels (Netherlands / Belgium)	Nightjet	14h / 13h 45m	Required
Innsbruck to Munich	EuroCity	1h 50m	Required

(Germany)			
Salzburg to Budapest (Hungary)	Railjet	5h 10m	Required
Salzburg / Innsbruck / Vienna to Zurich (Switzerland)	Railjet	5h 25m / 3h 30m / 7h 50m	Optional
Vienna to Budapest (Hungary)	EuroCity / Railjet	2h 40m	Optional (EuroCity) / Required (Railjet)
Vienna to Milan (Italy)	EuroNight	12h 25m (overnight)	Required
Vienna to Munich (Germany)	Railjet / Westbahn	4h	Optional
Vienna to Prague (Czech Republic)	Railjet / RegioJet	4h 30m	Required (Railjet) / Optional (RegioJet)
Vienna to Venice	EuroCity /	7h 45m / 10h	Required

(Italy)	EuroNight	40m (overnight)

Reservations

Reservations for ÖBB trains are not necessary. Trains for InterCity and EuroCity are optional if you want to ensure a decent seat. I suggest making a seat reservation during the busy summer season (May-September) and public holidays. Night trains need reservations. The cost of a night train depends on the sort of sleeping accommodation you choose.

How to Book Train Tickets in Austria

Reservations may be made for domestic and international high-speed trains, as well as night trains:

- Using our Reservation Service.
- Online on the ÖBB website (please note that bookings may only be made for domestic trains).
- At a ticket counter or self-service machine at a local rail station.
- By phone through the BB call center.
  +43 5 1717
  Availability: 24 hours a day, and in seven days a week

When you call, you'll hear a menu in German. Select extension "1" for train information and reservations. The BB booking center in Austria employs English-speaking personnel. The booking center may send your bookings to any nation of your choice without charging you a booking charge. The delivery fee is €5.

You may also pick up your bookings at major Austrian rail stations. Simply take your order number to a ticket counter at the station.

Austria Pass

- Use your whole holiday to see Austria by train.
- Standard pricing begins at $ 145.

Global Pass

- Have the flexibility to travel to Austria and up to 32 additional European countries.
- Standard pricing begins at $ 208.

Tricks & Tips

Quick facts

- Wien (local spelling: Wien) is the capital.
- Population: 8.4 million
- Language: German
- Currency: Euro (EUR)
- +43: dialing code

Austrian hub stations

Wien Westbahnhof (Vienna), Innsbruck Hbf, and Salzburg Hbf are the important hub stations in Austria. Trains to Austria's major cities and numerous international locations can be connected at these rail stations.

Station Facilities

Stations in Austria often offer good facilities, which frequently include:

- Luggage lockers
- Foreign exchange desks
- Restaurants and cafés
- ATM cash machines in tourist information offices
- Elevators and escalators
- Access for travelers with disabilities

Traveling by bus in Austria

As an added bonus, with an Austrian Eurail card, you receive free travel (pay just for the reservation) on the following bus routes:

- Klagenfurt - Graz
- Klagenfurt - Villach - Venice (Italy)
  (Venezia Mestre & Venezia Tronchetto)

Your Eurail Pass must be valid in both Austria and Italy for this trip.

Boat Trips in Austria

Eurail pass users can get cheap boat trips on various Austrian lakes and rivers

Turkey

Discover Turkey by rail, a patchwork of cultures with a hospitality tradition. With your Eurail pass, you can discover the variety of Istanbul, participate in one of the numerous action-packed outdoor experiences in Cappadocia, or relax on the gorgeous beaches of Antalya. Turkey is a traveler's dream. TCDD (Turkish Republic State Railways) runs passenger trains across the nation. The train is a convenient means to travel between cities like Istanbul, Ankara, and Izmir.

Route Maps

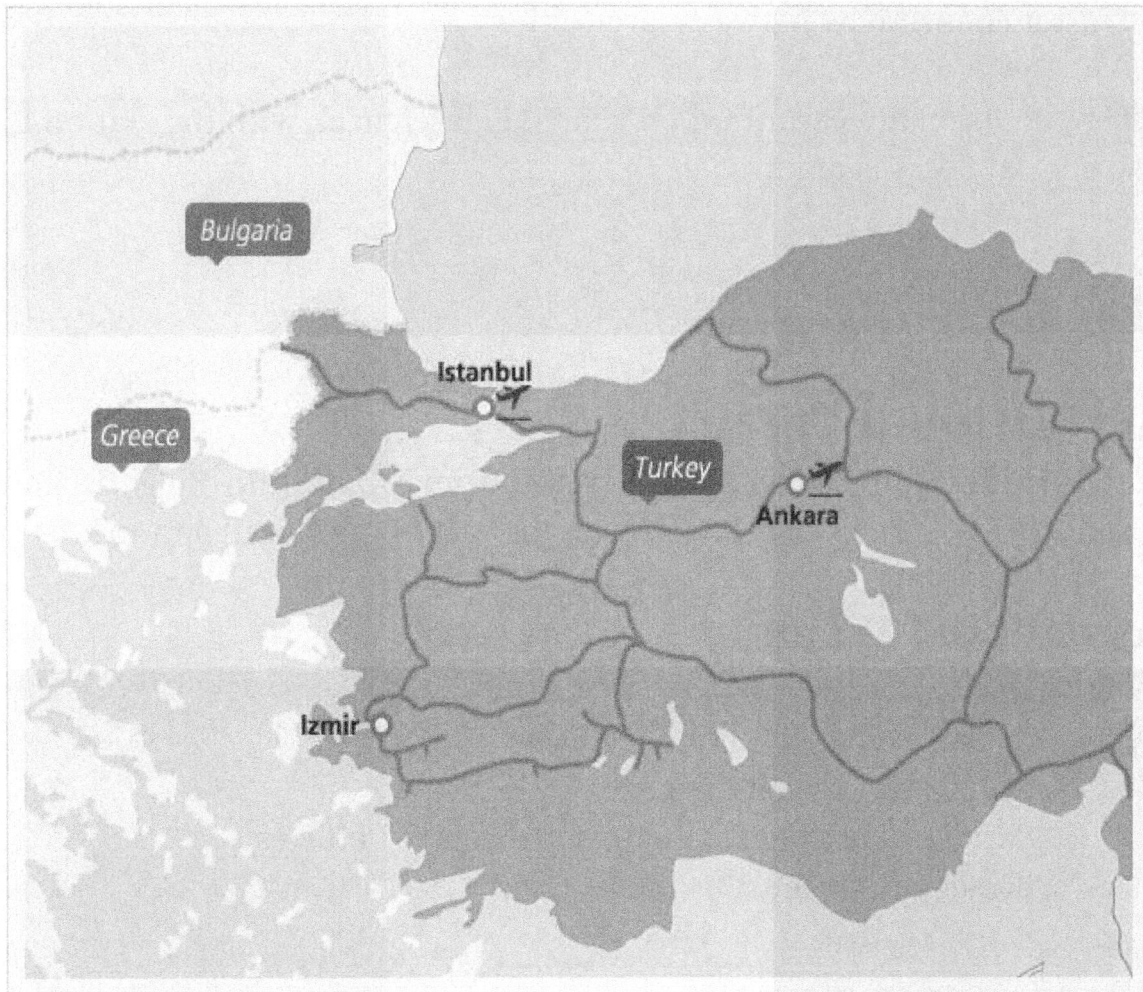

Trains in Turkey

TCDD (Turkish Republic State Railways) operates Turkey's rail network. Their trains traverse a huge portion of the country and link all major cities. Turkish rail timetables aren't always simple to locate online. Your best chance is to consult the Turkish version of the TCDD timetable at http://www.tcddtasimacilik.gov.tr/tren-sorgula/.

Domestic Trains

Regional trains (Bölgesel)
- Various routes around Turkey

The mainline train (Anahat)
- Faster connectivity between large cities

Bikes are occasionally permitted on trains. Please check with the station to see if a special ticket is required.

International Trains

Turkey provides daily international trains from Istanbul to Bulgaria and Romania, providing convenient access to the rest of the Eurail network.

International Trains
- Bosphorus Express
    - Istanbul Halkali - Plovdiv - Sofia
    - Runs every day of the year
    - Modern Turkish couchette and sleeping vehicles
    - Reservations must be made.

- Istanbul Halkali - Veliko Tarnovo -
  - Ruse - Bucharest
    - Only operates every day throughout the summer season (June 21st through October 9th).
    - Modern Turkish couchette and sleeping vehicles
    - Reservations must be made.

The train from Istanbul to Bucharest and Sofia departs at Istanbul Halkali station. The metro/Marmaray train is the most convenient method to get here. It stretches from the city's eastern side, under the Bosphorus strait, to the city's western side, and ends in Halkali. Eurail Passes are not usable on Marmaray trains.

High-Speed
- YHT (Yüksek Hzl) high-speed train
- An expanding network of high-speed lines
- Modern trains are capable of reaching speeds of up to 250 km/h
- The following lines are presently operational:
  - Istanbul - Eskişehir - Ankara
  - Istanbul - Eskişehir - Konya - Karaman
  - Ankara - Konya - Karaman
  - Ankara - Sivas

YHT trains now serve five stations in the Istanbul metro area: Halkal, Bakrköy, Söütlüçeşme, Bostanc, and Pendik. Bakrköy and Söütlüçeşme are the closest to the city center and are well-served by metro and suburban (Marmaray) trains.

Night Trains
Turkey has an extensive network of night trains that reach all regions of the nation. Trains have contemporary air-conditioned cars with luxurious

Pullman seats, sleepers, and couchettes. Make reservations in advance, since trains often sell out.

- Ankara Ekspresi
  - Istanbul - Eskişehir - Ankara
  - When the High-Speed Trains (YHT) are sold out, this is a good option.
- Daily Dögü Ekspresi
  - Ankara - Kayseri - Sivas - Erzincan
    - Erzurum - Kars
  - The Eufrates River route is quite picturesque.
- Daily Vangölü
  - Ankara - Kayseri - Sivas - Malatya
    - Elazig - Tatvan
  - Across the enormous Lake Van, take a ferry to Van.
  - Twice a week
- Güney Kurtalan
  - Ankara - Kayseri - Sivas - Malatya
    - Diyarbakir - Batman - Kurtalan
  - 5 times each week
- Blue Night Train (Mavi Tren)
  - Ankara - Izmir
  - Konya to Izmir
  - Daily

*In addition to the Dou Ekspresi, there is another train called the 'Turistik Dou Ekspresi'. This train is not valid for pass holders.

Popular connections
Domestic Routes

Here are the typical travel times between Turkey's major cities. Reservations are strongly advised for any of these rail journeys.

Route	Travel time
Istanbul to Ankara (YHT)	4h 30m
Ankara to Izmir (Night train)	12h 35m
Istanbul to Izmir*	9h
Istanbul to Konya (YHT)	4h 45m

Ankara to Kars (Dogu Express)	26h 30m
Ankara to Van (Vangölü Express)	26h 45m
Ankara to Konya (YHT)	1h 45m
Ankara to Sivas (YHT)	2h 30m

*(across the Sea of Marmara) You'll need to take a ferry from Istanbul to Bandirma, From there, in 6 hours, the train will take you to Izmir

International Routes

Route	Which train?	Travel time	Reservations
Istanbul to Bucharest (Romania)	Bosphorus Express	13h 35m	Required

Istanbul to Sofia (Bulgaria)	Bosphorus Express	21h 10m	Required

Reservations

It is not possible to make a reservation using the Eurail reservation self-service system.
locally at the train station

Good to know

High-speed (YHT) and night trains need reservations, which may only be made at Turkish railway stations. They usually sell out, so make a reservation a few days in advance.

Turkey Pass

- Spend your whole holiday visiting Turkey by train.
- Standard pricing begins at $ 59.

Global Pass

- You are free to visit Turkey as well as the other 32 European countries.
- Standard pricing begins at $ 211.

Tips & Tricks for Turkey

Cross Turkey's biggest lake

With a Eurail card valid in Turkey, you may take a ferry trip for €2 on the following route (no reservation required):

- Tatvan-Van (only on Tuesdays and Fridays)

Quick facts

- Ankara is the capital city.
- 75.6 million people
- Language: Turkish
- Currency: Turkish Lira (TRY)
- Dialing code: +90

Great Britain

Over twenty distinct private rail firms operate the rail network in the United Kingdom. Your Interrail pass makes train travel in the United Kingdom incredibly easy.

Route Maps

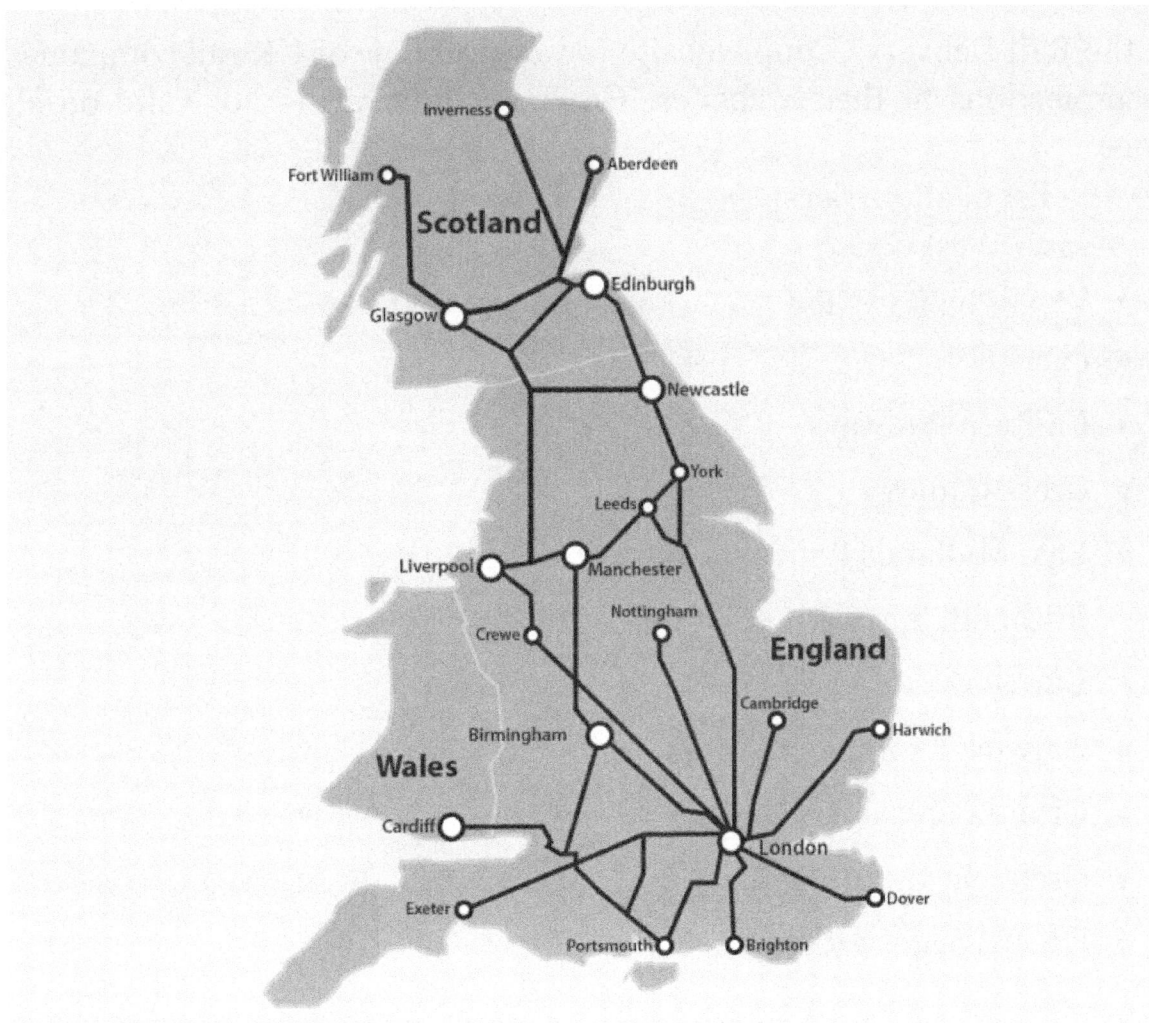

Train types

Domestic trains
Rail network

Visitors visiting the United Kingdom will find it simple to travel across England, Scotland, and Wales because of the huge and well-developed rail system. With about 20,000 train runs on a normal workday, Britain's rail network crisscrosses the country, providing services to even tiny towns and villages. For general travel information, go to www.nationalrail.co.uk.

Visit the Rail Delivery Group website for an overview of UK rail companies and connections to their websites. However, Interrail is not valid on all airlines.

Below is a list of all carriers:
- Avanti West Coast
  - Caledonian Sleeper
  - c2c
  - Chiltern Railways
  - Cross Country
  - East Midlands Railway
  - Elizabeth line
  - Eurostar
  - Gatwick Express
  - Grand Central
  - Great Northern
  - Great Western Railway;

  (Including Night Riviera sleeper)

  - Greater Anglia
  - Hull Trains

- Island Line
- LNER
- London Northwestern Railway
- London Overground
- Lumo
- Merseyrail
- National Rail
- Northern
- ScotRail
- Southeastern
- Southern
- South Western Railway
- Stansted Express
- Thameslink
- TransPennine Express
- Transport for Greater Manchester
- Transport for Wales
- West Midlands Railway

International rail service

Eurostar (ES)

- The Eurostar connects London to Paris (France), Brussels (Belgium), and Amsterdam (The Netherlands).
- Reservations are mandatory.

Night Trains

Caledonian Sleeper
- Night Trains run on the following routes:

- London Euston - Edinburgh - Aberdeen
- London Euston - Edinburgh - Glasgow
- - Fort William
- London Euston - Inverness

Night Riviera Sleeper

Runs the following route:
- London Paddington - Plymouth - Penzance.

Popular connections
Domestic routes
Main stations and connections

London Euston

Trains to Birmingham, Edinburgh, Glasgow, Holyhead, Liverpool, Manchester, and Newcastle

London King's Cross

Trains from London King's Cross to Cambridge, Dundee, Edinburgh, Glasgow, Leeds, Newcastle, and York.

London Paddington

Trains from London Paddington to Bristol, Cardiff, Exeter, Oxford, Penzance, and Plymouth.

You may use your Interrail Pass on the Elizabeth Line (by TfL) to travel between Paddington and Heathrow Airport.

London Victoria

Trains to Brighton, Dover, Portsmouth, and Southampton

London Waterloo

Trains to Exeter, Portsmouth, Southampton, Weymouth, and Windsor

Liverpool Lime Street

Trains to London, Manchester, and Glasgow

Manchester Piccadilly

Trains to London, Birmingham, Cardiff, Liverpool, and Glasgow

Birmingham New Street

Trains to London, Manchester, Liverpool, Bristol, and Penzance

Reservations

Reservation system for intercity trains
>   Interrail
>> • Eurostar (International tickets) Only

Administration fees apply when booking via Interrail self-service.

- EUR 2,- per person per train
- Additional € 9,- per order
  (for paper tickets)

With railway carriers

- **SNCB (b-europe):** Only Eurostar trains.
- **LNER (London North Eastern Railway):** Domestic trains
- **ACP Rail:** Domestic trains
- **GWR (Great Western Railway):** Domestic day trains
- **Caledonian Sleeper:** Domestic night train (Seat reservations must be made via the Guest Service Centre).
- Railtourguide (a travel agency located in the United Kingdom)

In the United Kingdom, at a rail station

Good to know

Eurostar: Every customer with a Global Pass will be able to travel on the Eurostar (between London and Paris, London and Brussels, and London and Amsterdam/Rotterdam) with a mandatory reservation. Note that the Interrail Great Britain Pass is not valid on Eurostar. Reservations in the United Kingdom may be made online at ACP Rail (€6) or locally for free. LNER reservations are free.

Reservations for Eurostar may be made via the
- Eurail Reservation Service.
- The Rail Planner App
- b-europe.com.
- Call the Eurostar booking line at (+44) 01233617575 (outside the UK) or (+44) 03432186186 (inside the UK).
- Directly at Eurostar terminals.

Bicycles are normally permitted on British trains, however, rules vary by company.

Reservations are required.
- Eurostar
- Caledonian Sleeper
- Night Riviera Sleeper

There is no need to make reservations.
- Avanti West Coast
- c2c
- Chiltern Railways
- Cross Country (Recommended)
- East Midlands Railway
- Elizabeth's line
- Gatwick Express
- Grand Central
- Great Northern
- Great Western Railway (Recommended)

- Greater Anglia
- Hull Trains
- Island Line
- London Northwestern Railway
- LNER
- London Overground
- Lumo
- Merseyrail
- National Rail
- Northern
- ScotRail
- Southeastern
- Southern
- South Western Railway
- Stansted Express
- Thameslink
- TransPennine Express
- Transport for Greater Manchester
- Transport for Wales
- West Midlands Railway

Great Britain Pass

Global Pass for Great Britain.

The Interrail Global Pass is a versatile and cost-effective option to travel across up to 33 European countries. Travel by rail from one exciting place to the next. One day you're on a pub crawl around Amsterdam, the next you're white-water rafting in Interlaken, Switzerland.

Interrail Great Britain Pass

The Interrail Great Britain Pass is an excellent way to experience all that Great Britain has to offer. Travel comfortably from city to city and experience the local bars, wonderful sights and more.

Croatia

Croatia's railway network (HZ Putniki Prijevoz) is centered around Zagreb. Croatia is strategically located to serve as an intersection for routes connecting Europe's west-to-east and north to south.

Routes Map

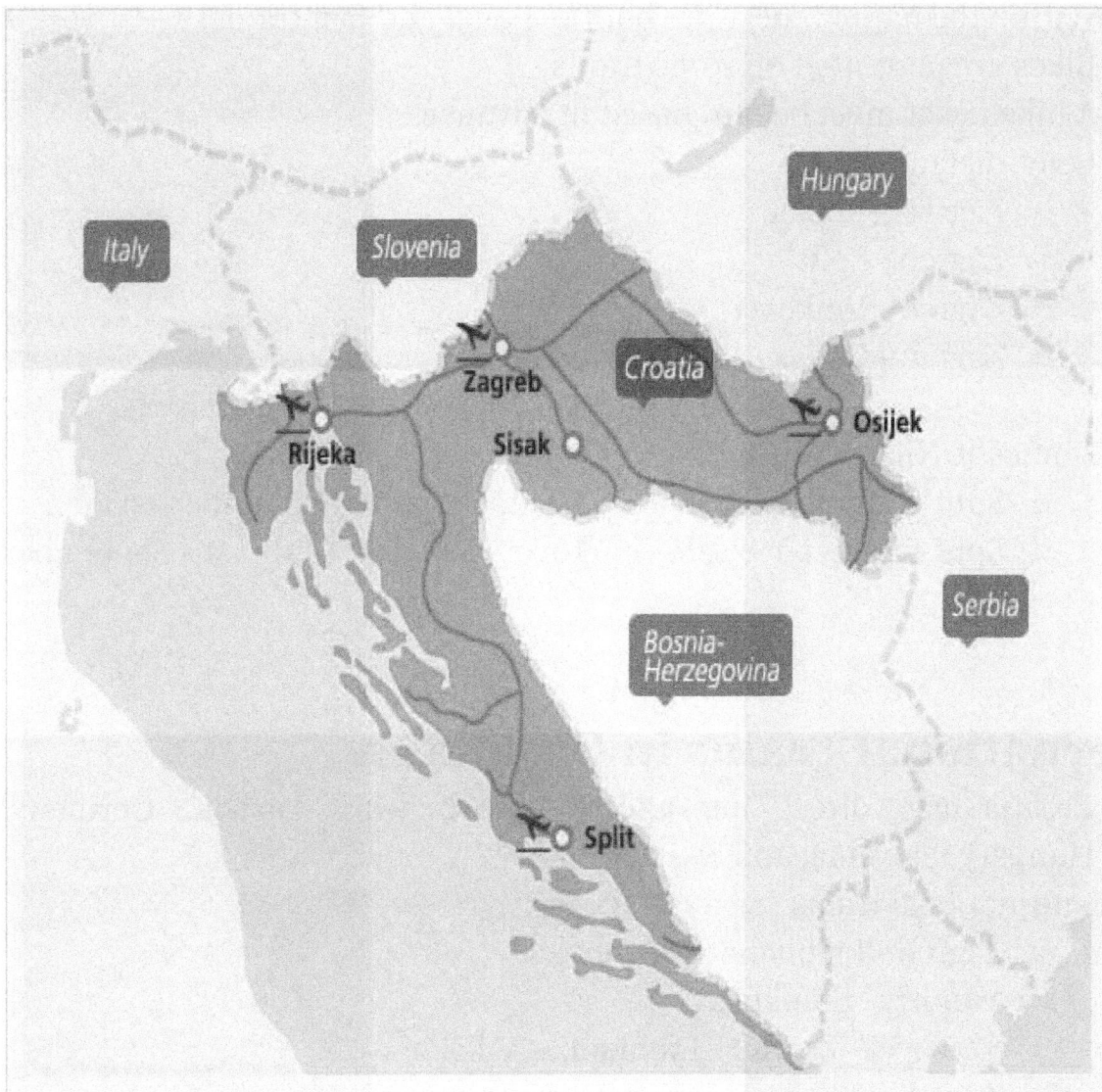

Train types in Croatia

Hrvatske eljeznice (HZ) manages Croatia's national rail network. You may use the Interrail timetable to check train timings. Some Croatian cities, such as Zadar, are not listed in the timetable. Instead, see the HZ timetable at www.hzpp.hr/en

Domestic Trains in Croatia
- The HZ links the majority of Croatia's main cities.
- Within the nation, there are both regional and fast trains.
- Bikes are permitted on some trains.
- A bike ticket must be purchased in advance.
- Long-distance trains
  - Zagreb - Rijeka
  - Zagreb - Split
  - Zagreb - Vinkovci
  - Zagreb - Osijek

- Domestic Night Trains
  - Split - Zagreb - Osijek (Mon-Sat, July 1st - September 1st)
  - Split - Zagreb - Sisak - Vinkovci - Vukovar (July 1st - September 1st)

International Trains in Croatia
- Croatia has direct international links with Austria, Germany, Hungary, Slovenia, and Switzerland.
- International trains
  - Zagreb - Ljubljana - Salzburg - Munich - Frankfurt
  - Vinkovci - Zagreb - Ljubljana - Villach
  - Zagreb - Maribor - Graz - Vienna
  - Zagreb - Siófok - Budapest Delí
- International night trains

- Zagreb - Salzburg - Munich - Stuttgart
- Zagreb - Zurich
- Rijeka - Munich - Stuttgart
- Split - Zagreb - Vienna - Bratislava (June 22nd - September 2nd)
- Split - Budapest Keleti (Not every day. (June 20th - 22nd September)
- Split-Prague (Regiojet) is not eligible for passholders.

Popular Connections

Domestic Routes

What are the rail travel times between Croatia's largest cities? If you utilize regional trains on the following routes, you will not need to make reservations:

Route	Travel time	Reservations
Zagreb to Split	6h 30m	Required
Zagreb to Osijek	5h 30m	Optional
Zagreb to Rijeka	4h 24m	Not possible

Zagreb to Sisak	50m	Optional
Zagreb to Vinkovci	4h 15m	Optional

The InterCity train from Zagreb to Split takes 6.5 hours while the Night Train takes 8 hours. Reservations are necessary for both trips.

To go to Dubrovnik, take the train to Split and then a bus.

Reservations

Interrail reservation self-service system
  - Interrail
  - International only: IC, EC, Nightjet, and Euro Night

Administration fees apply when booking via Interrail self-service.
  - EUR 2,- per person per train
  - Additional € 9,- per order
  - (for paper tickets)

With ÖBB (Austrian Railways): Domestic and foreign trains
Locally in Croatia, at the rail station

Good to know
Reservations are needed for the following Intercity train routes:
(IC) Zagreb - Split

Croatia Pass

Interrail Croatia Pass
- Get extensive rail travel in Croatia.
- There are discounts for
- children, seniors, and families.
- Additional benefits include a 20% discount on ferry voyages between Split and Ancona, Italy.
- Prices begin at € 54.

Interrail Global Pass

- Train travel is available in up to 33 European countries, including Croatia.
- There are discounts for
- children, seniors, and families.
- Additional benefits include a 20% discount on ferry voyages between Split and Ancona, Italy.
- Prices begin at € 194.

Croatian Tips & Tricks

Croatia's major rail station
- Zagreb's central station is known as the Zagrebacki Glavni Kolodvor.
- To get to the station from Zagreb Airport, take a bus to the city terminal, then a tram to the central rail station.
- Interrail Passes are not usable on buses or trams.

Poland

Grab your Eurail Pass and board your train for a magnificent East European rail journey. From Warsaw to Wroclaw, Kraków to Toru, the people and sites of Poland are remarkable. Get a taste of this east European treasure's legendary hospitality and affordability by taking advantage of the efficient and accessible Polish train service.

Routes Map

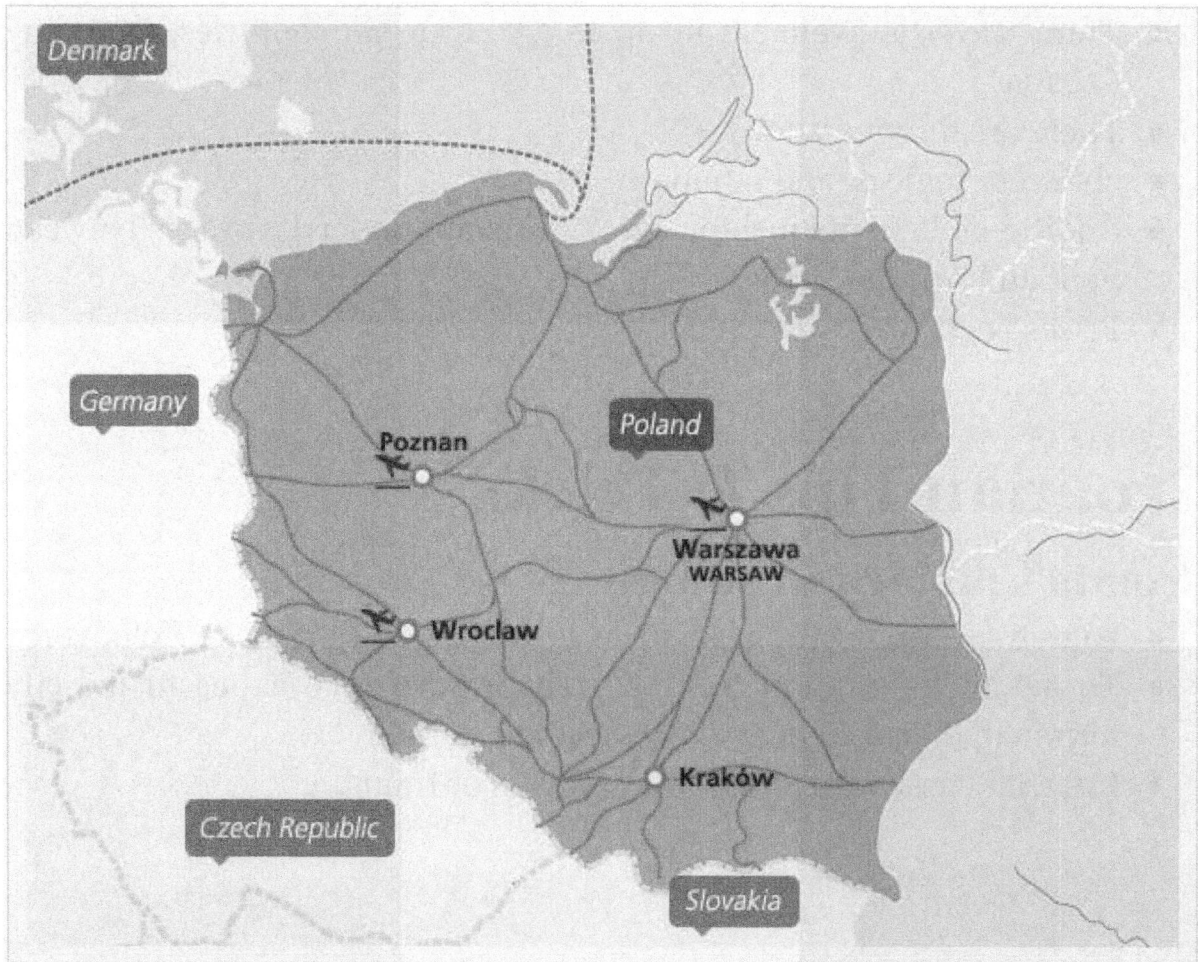

Train types in Poland

Intercity trains in Poland

- The majority of passenger trains in Poland are operated by PKP Intercity and the Polish State Railways.

Express InterCity Premium (EIP)

- Operates on an important North-South corridor:
    - Gdánsk-Warsaw-Krakow/Katowice/Wroclaw
- Speeds of up to 200 km/h
- Reservations with a supplement are required (costs are 43 PLN / 10 EUR).
- A supplement is necessary.
- Popular trains; reserve your seat well in advance.

Express InterCity (EIC)

- Operates on vital domestic routes
- Speeds of up to 160 km/h
- The most luxury and modern intercity rolling stock
- Reservations for seats are strongly advised.

Intercity (IC) and Twoje Linie Kolejowe (TLK)

- Connect significant cities in Poland
- Day and nightly services are provided.
- Intercity.pl contains a list of IC and TLK connections.
- Seat reservations (1,00 PLN) are required for some trains.
    - In the schedule, these trains are denoted by the letter [R].
- Seat reservations are recommended on other IC and TLK trains (seating cars).
- Regional trains in Poland

POLREGIO (Przewozy Regionalne)

- **REGIO (R)**
    - Local trains stop at every station along their itineraries.
    - Only second class.

     ○ There is no need for a reservation.

InterRegio (IR)

- Operates on the Lódz to Warsaw route, stopping at medium and major stations along the way.
- Only second class.
- There is no need for a reservation.

InterREGIO (IR)

- Operates on the Lódz to Warsaw route, stopping at medium and major station along the way.
- Only second class.
- There is no need for a reservation.

Koleje Dolnoslaskie (OS)

- Lower Silesian Railways.
- Regional trains operate throughout southwestern Poland.
- There is no need for a reservation.
- Please keep in mind that the Kulturzug, the direct train between Wroclaw (Breslaw) and Berlin, is not included.

PKP Szybka Kolej Miejska w Trójmieście Sp. z o.o.

- SKM in Trójmieście is an alternate name.
- Regional trains operate in Poland's Tricity region (Gdask - Sopot - Gdynia - Rumia - Reda - Wejherowo - Lębork).
- There is no need for a reservation.

International trains in Poland

EuroCity (EC) and Intercity (IC)

- International trains run on important lines linking Poland to cities in neighboring countries.
- Reservations must be made in advance.
- Routes that are presently active:

- o Warsaw - Poznan - Berlin
- o Warsaw - Katowice - Ostrava - Prague
- o Gdánsk - Bydgoszcz - Poznan - Berlin
- o Przemysl - Krakow - Katowice
  - Wroclaw - Berlin
- o Przemysl - Krakow - Katowice - Ostrava - Prague
- o Przemysl - Krakow - Katowice -
  - Vienna - Graz
- o Terespol - Warsaw - Katowice
  - Bratislava - Budapest
- o Krakow - Warsaw - Mockava -
  - Kaunas - Vilnius

The international service Krakow-Vilnius is divided in Mockava:
- A Polish rail connects Krakow, Warsaw, and Mockava.
- A Lithuanian train travels from Mockava to Kaunas and then to Vilnius.

Seat bookings are presently only available online for the Polish part of the train till the border stop Trakiszki.

Regional and international linkages
- International trains on regional lines link Poland to cities in neighboring countries such as Germany, the Czech Republic, and Slovakia.
- A reservation in advance is not feasible.

Leo Express
- Twice a week, numerous Polish cities are served.
- Krakow - Katowice - Ostrava - Prague
- Reservations are necessary, but they are free.

RegioJet Bus
- RegioJet, established in the Czech Republic, operates a link bus service from Krakow and Katowice to Ostrava (Czech Republic), with

a guaranteed change to RegioJet trains in the direction of Olomouc and Prague, as well as the Kosice and Tatra mountains in Slovakia.
- The RegioJet bus also is included in the Interrail Global Pass.
- Reservations are needed (€3 per seat for 1st and 2nd Class Pass holders) and may be booked online at regiojet.com/our-tickets/interrail.

Domestic night trains in Poland
- Domestic Overnight trains
- Conects major cities in Poland.
- You must arrange overnight accommodations or a seat on this train in advance.
- Routes that are presently active:
  - Warsaw - Szczecin - Swinoujscie
  - Warsaw - Wroclaw - Jelenia Gora
  - Swinoujscie - Szczecin - Krakow - Przemysl
  - Gdynia - Gdansk - Krakow
  - Gdynia - Gdansk - Warsaw - Zakopane
  - Szczecin - Poznan - Zakopane (summer only)
  - Hel - Gdynia - Gdansk - Krakow (summer only)

International night trains in Poland
Euro Night (EN)
- International overnight trains.
- Connects Poland to Germany, the Czech Republic, Hungary, and Austria.
- You must arrange overnight accommodations or a seat on this train in advance.
- Routes that are presently active:
  - Warsaw - Krakow - Katowice - Bratislava - Budapest
  - Warsaw - Krakow - Katowice - Vienna - Graz

- Berlin - Rzepin - Wroclaw -
  Vienna - Graz
- Berlin - Rzepin - Wroclaw -
  Bratislava - Budapest

RegioJet

- International nighttime trains.
- Connects Poland to the Czech Republic.
- You must arrange overnight accommodations or a seat on this train in advance.
- Passholders presently have access to the following routes:
  - Przemysl - Krakow - Katowice - Prague

Private Railway
Private rail companies in Poland

Arriva RP

- Operating in central-northern Poland.
- With rail pass you will not be allow to board these trains.

SKM and WKD

- Commuter rails operating the Warsaw region.
- A rail pass will not allow you to board these trains.

Popular Connections

Domestic routes

Here are estimated train timetables between Poland's most populous cities:

Route	Which train?	Duration	Reservations
Warsaw to Krakow	EIP / EIC / IC / TLK	2h 30m / 4h	Required / Recommended
Warsaw to Wroclaw	EIP / EIC / IC / TLK	3h 30m / 4h 30m	Required / Recommended
Warsaw to Gdansk	EIP / EIC / IC / TLK	2h 30m / 3h 10m	Required / Recommended
Warsaw to Poznan	EIP / IC / TLK	2h 30m / 3h	Required / Recommended

Warsaw to Katowice	EIP / EIC / IC / TLK	2h 30m / 3h	Required / Recommended
Wrocław to Sczcecin	EIC / IC	5h 20m / 5h 50m	Required / Recommended
Krakow to Wrocław	IC / TLK	3h	Required / Recommended
Krakow to Gdansk	EIP / EIC / IC / TLK	5h	Required / Recommended
Krakow to Poznan	IC / TLK	5h	Required / Recommended
Warsaw to	IC	2h 40m	Required

Olsztyn			
Szczecin to Gdánsk	IC	4h 40m	Required
Wroclaw to Gdánsk	IC / TLK	5h	Required / Recommended

International Routes

Modern, air-conditioned international trains connect Poland to prominent cities in the following European countries:

Route	Which train?	Duration	Reservations
Warsaw to Berlin (Germany)	EuroCity	5h 50m	Required
Warsaw to Budapest (Hungary)	EuroCity / Euro Night	11h 25m / 12h 50m (overnight)	Required

Warsaw to Prague (Czech Republic)	EuroCity	8h 30m (overnight)	Required
Warsaw to Vienna (Austria)	EuroCity / Euro Night	7h 15m / 11h 10m (overnight)	Required
Wrocław to Dresden (Germany)	*trilex* regional train	4h	Not required

Reservations

How can I book rail tickets in Poland?

Reservation system for Eurail

- Eurail
- TLK, IC, EC, EIC, Nightjet, Euro Night

Booking via Eurail self-service costs administrative fees.

- EUR 2,- per person per train
- Additional € 9,- per order (for paper tickets)

With railway carriers

- PKP Intercity (Polish railways): Domestic trains
- CD (Czech railways): Domestic and international trains
- ÖBB (Austrian Railways): Domestic and international trains
- Leo Express: Domestic and international trains (only Leo Express)
- RegioJet: International trains (only RegioJet)

Other platforms
- Polrail: Domestic and international trains

Locally in Poland, at the rail station

Seat bookings made at Polish train stations cost 1 Zloty per seat, the same as on the PKP Intercity (Polish railroads) website. EIP trains still demand an additional supplement.
Intercity.pl provides information about official selling points.

By phone
By contacting +49 1806 996 633 (open 24/7).

Good to know
PKP Intercity
- EIP - a seat reservation (43,00 PLN) is required (this includes the supplement fee).
- EIC - a seat reservation (1,00 PLN) is advised.
- Seat reservations (1,00 PLN) are required for some IC and TLK trains.
  - Intercity.pl has a list of these links.
  - In the timetable, these trains are marked [R].
  - Seat reservations are recommended on other IC and TLK trains (seating cars).

Seat bookings are not available for POLREGIO, PKP SKM, or Koleje Dolnoslaskie.
Detailed information on rules for reserving seats in Poland can be obtained on the PKP Intercity website (intercity.pl).

Poland Pass

- Make the most of your holiday by seeing Poland by train.
- Standard pricing begin at $ 59.

Global Pass

- You are free to tour Poland and up to 32 other Europeon countries.
- Standard pricing begins at $ 211.

Poland Tips and Techniques

Bus travel to Germany or the Czech Republic

If your Eurail pass is valid in Poland, Germany, or the Czech Republic, you may travel for free on the following routes (pay just the reservation fee):

- Krakow - Wroclaw - Berlin (Germany)
- Krakow - Katowice - Ostrava (Czech Republic)

Quick Facts

- Warsaw (local spelling: Warszawa) is the capital.
- Population: 38.2 million
- Language: Polish
- Currency: Polish Zloty (PLN)
- +48: digit dialing code

Netherlands

Travel by train across the Netherlands with a Eurail pass, from the easygoing city of Amsterdam to historic places like Utrecht and Maastricht. Consider seeing the Keukenhof flower gardens and the Zaanse Schans traditional residences when in the Netherlands. Visit tulip fields along the route as the train takes you to every part of this tiny but interesting nation.

Route Maps

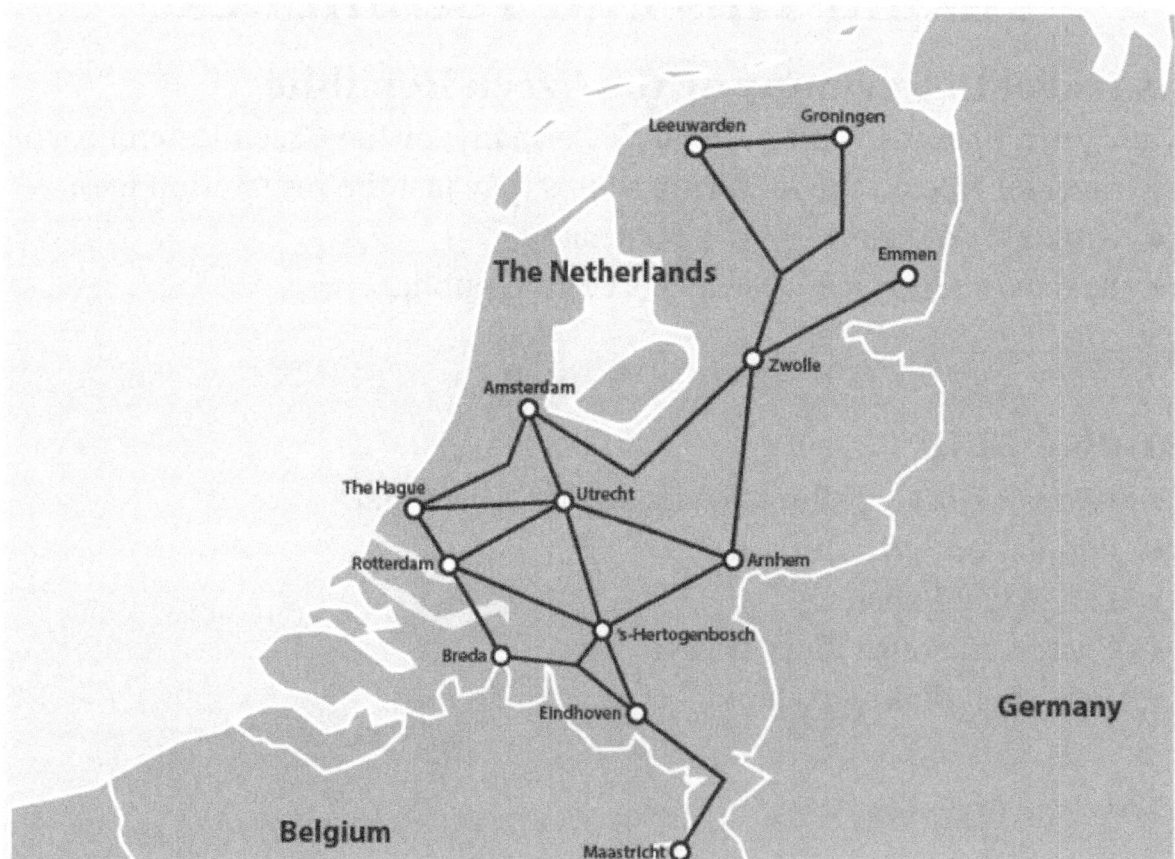

Train Types

Domestic Train

INTERNATIONAL NIGHT
Regional and intercity trains in the Netherlands
Intercity (IC)
- Connects important cities such as Amsterdam, Maastricht, and Utrecht.
- There is no need for a reservation.

Sprinter (RE)
- These trains, which are slower than Intercity trains, connect rural locations to bigger Dutch cities.
- There is no need for a reservation.

Domestic high-speed trains in the Netherlands
Intercity Direct (ICD)
- This train travels quicker between Amsterdam Centraal, Schiphol Airport, Rotterdam Centraal, and Breda.
- A supplement of € 2,90 is needed between Schiphol Airport and Rotterdam Centraal.
- An Intercity Direct (ICD) supplement is only needed if this train is utilized for domestic journey.

International high-speed trains in the Netherlands
ICE (ICE)
- Connects Amsterdam to Frankfurt (Germany) and Basel (Switzerland).
- Reservations are required during the summer season (June 17th till August 18th).
- During the remainder of the year, bookings are optional but strongly suggested.

- Amsterdam-Basel trains will only operate till Frankfurt between May 27th and September 12th.

Intercity Berlin (IC)
- From Amsterdam, it takes 6 hours 20 minutes to get to Berlin.
- Reservations are strictly optional. When traveling during a busy season, I suggest making a reservation.

Intercity Brussels (IC)
- Connects Amsterdam and Rotterdam to Brussels (Belgium).
- Reservations are not necessary.
- An Intercity Direct (ICD) supplement is only needed if this train is utilized for domestic travel.

Eurostar (EST)
- High-speed trains run over the following lines to Belgium, France, and the United Kingdom:
  - Amsterdam - Schiphol - Rotterdam - Antwerp - Brussels - Paris
  - Amsterdam - Schiphol - Rotterdam - Antwerp - Brussels - Disneyland Paris
  - Amsterdam - Rotterdam - London

Reservations are required for certain trains, which might be completely booked. I suggest booking your reservation as soon as possible to prevent disappointment.

- Former Thalys trains in red provide services to Brussels and (Disney) Paris.

Popular connections

Domestic routes

The following are estimated train timetables between Holland's most populous cities. These routes are all accessible by Intercity trains and are free for holders of a Eurail Pass valid in the Netherlands.

Route	Duration
Amsterdam to Groningen	2h 10m
Amsterdam to Leeuwarden	2h 10m
Amsterdam to Maastricht	2h 30m
Amsterdam to Rotterdam	40m
Amsterdam to Schiphol Airport	15m

Amsterdam to The Hague	50m
Amsterdam to Utrecht	27m

International routes

Popular European cities from which to travel to and from the Netherlands

Route	Which train?	Duration	Reservations
Amsterdam to Berlin (Germany)	Intercity Berlin	6h 20m	Optional
Amsterdam to Düsseldorf (Germany)	ICE	2h 10m	Optional (Required June 17th till August 18th)
Amsterdam to Frankfurt (Germany)	ICE	4h	Optional (Required June 17th till August 18th)
Amsterdam to	ICE	6h 40m	Optional

Basel (Switzerland) Only till Düsseldorf between May 27th and September 12th			(Required June 17th till August 18th)
Amsterdam to Paris (France)	Eurostar	3h 20m	Required
Amsterdam to Brussels (Belgium)	Intercity Brussels	2h 50m	Not required
Amsterdam to London (Great Britain)	Eurostar	4h 50m	Required
Amsterdam to Vienna / Innsbruck (Austria)	ÖBB Nightjet	13h 45m (overnight)	Required
Amsterdam to Zürich (Switzerland)	ÖBB Nightjet	11h 35m (overnight)	Required
Rotterdam (via Amsterdam) to	European Sleeper	9h 30m (overnight)	Required

Berlin
(Germany)

Reservations

Reservation system for Eurail
- Eurail
- Eurostar, TGV, IC Berlin, ICE, Nightjet

Booking via Eurail self-service costs administrative fees.
- EUR 2,- per person per train
- Additional € 9,- per order (for paper tickets)

With railway carriers
- SNCB (b-europe): Only Eurostar
- DB (German Railways): International trains to Germany/Switzerland
  - IC, ICE

ÖBB (Austrian Railways): International trains to Germany/Austria/Switzerland
  - IC, ICE, and Nightjet
  CD (Czech railways): International trains to Germany/Austria/Switzerland
- IC, ICE, and Nightjet

- European Sleeper: Only European Sleeper trains, international

By contacting NS International Customer Service
- +31 030 2300023 (open 24/7). The contact center is only open for questions from 11 p.m. to 7 a.m.

- When you call, you'll hear a menu in Dutch. Choose extension '5' for English-language services. NS International may reserve trains in many European countries (€7.50 booking charge per passenger, with a maximum of €22.50 per order; 2 bookings per call permitted or 1 consecutive journeys). Reservations made over the phone may be paid for using iDEAL, Mastercard, Visa, American Express, Bancontact, or SOFORT. Your reservation ticket will be sent to you. You may put it into the NS International app or print it by following a link in the email.

Locally, at one of the five NS International ticket counters in the Netherlands.

- NS International ticket counters can be found at Amsterdam Central Station, Arnhem Central Station, Rotterdam Central Station, Schiphol Airport, and Utrecht Central Station.

Note that Eurostar trains are popular and, as a result, frequently sell out rapidly. Make sure you obtain your seat reservation in advance. To identify trains without seat reservations in the timetable, toggle the 'no reservation required' option.

Netherlands Pass

- Discover Belgium, the Netherlands, and Luxembourg by train.
- Standard pricing start at $ 120.

Global Pass

- You are free to travel the Netherlands and up to 32 other European countries.
- Standard pricing begin at $ 211.

Pass benefits

Ferry crossings to the United Kingdom are discounted.
Discounted ferry travel is an additional advantage of a Eurail pass valid in the Netherlands on the route:

- Hoek van Holland - Harwich (Great Britain)

Access to NS International lounges

Eurail first-class card holders get free access to the NS International lounges at the following train stations:

- Amsterdam Centraal
- Rotterdam Centraal
- Schiphol

Tips & Tricks for the Netherlands

What are the important rail stations in the Netherlands?

The three major hubs of the Netherlands provide links to many domestic and international destinations. They are:

- Amsterdam Central Station
- Rotterdam Central Station
- Utrecht Central Station

The railway stations in the Netherlands are very well built, with great facilities:

- Lockers to store your belongings
- Cash machines and foreign exchange desks
- Cafés, restaurants, and stores
- Tourist information offices
- Elevators, escalators, and disable access

Dutch hub stations

The major hub stations in the Netherlands are Amsterdam Centraal, Rotterdam Centraal, and Utrecht Centraal. Trains to the Netherlands' major cities and numerous overseas locations can be boarded at these rail stations.

Please be aware that the Dutch Railways have blocked the entrance gates to numerous Dutch stations. To enter the station, check for the square barcode on your Eurail pass cover. Hold the barcode against the scanner next to an entrance gate, and the gate will open for you.

Bicycles aboard trains in the Netherlands

Cycling short distances while using the nation's efficient trains between towns and cities is one of the greatest methods to discover the country. Cycling is quite popular in the Netherlands. Most major rail stations provide bike rental services.

Names are spelled differently in the Netherlands.

On rail schedules and at train stations in the Netherlands, you'll normally see the local spelling of Dutch cities.

Good to know:
- Centraal Station = Central Station
- Den Haag = The Hague
- Hoek van Holland = Hook of Holland

Quick facts
- Amsterdam is the capital city.
- Population: 16.8 million
- Language: Dutch
- Currency: Euro (EUR)
- dialing code: +31

Ireland

Traveling by rail in Ireland offers you the best of the two worlds. The Republic of Ireland has attractive green scenery, a lively capital city, iconic castles, and lovely pubs. Northern Ireland's magnificent coastline, history, and dynamic city Belfast may all be explored.

Routes Map

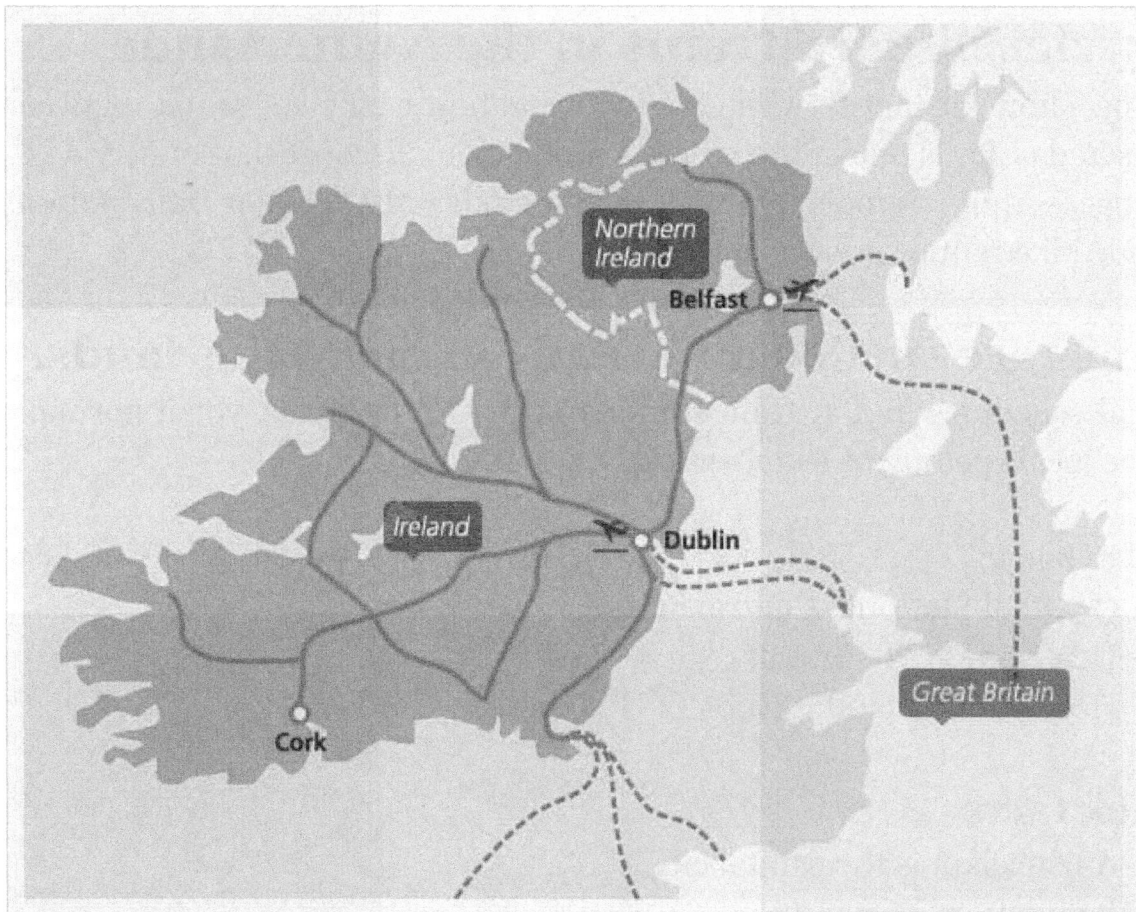

Train types in Ireland

Iarnrod Éireann (Irish Rail) operates trains in Ireland. Northern Ireland Railways (NI Railways) is in charge of rail services in Northern Ireland.

Trains in the Republic of Ireland Iarnród Éireann (Irish Rail) operates modern and dependable trains across the nation, with several connections to and from Dublin. Start planning your vacation using the Irish Rail schedules and travel planner at irishrail.ie.

- Your Interrail Pass is applicable on InterCity trains: Rail services that are quick and of excellent quality that link popular cities and communities in the Republic of Ireland. WiFi is accessible on the majority of connections.
- DART (Dublin Area Rapid Transport): Dublin's electric train system. Simply present your Pass at the ticket booth to enter the gates.

Northern Ireland Trains

Northern Ireland train times are available on the NI Railway (Translink) website.
All NI Railway trains have free wifi.
Bicycles are permitted on trains after 9.30 a.m. at no additional cost.

Scenic Routes

Republic of Ireland
Rosslare - Waterford/Rosslare -
Rosslare- Wexford - Enniscorthy - Wicklow - Greystones - Dun Laoghaire

Northern Ireland
Londonderry - Coleraine

Republic of Ireland

Most long-distance services begin or conclude in Dublin. Intercity trains operate these services. The Enterprise Service travels from Dublin to Belfast in slightly over two hours.

Route	Travel time (by InterCity)
Dublin Connolly to Belfast *Enterprise Service*	2h 15m
Dublin Heuston to Cork	2h 35m
Dublin Heuston to Waterford	2h 10m
Dublin Heuston to Limerick (Via Limerick Junction)	2h 05m
Waterford to Limerick	2h 30m

(Via Limerick Junction)

Limerick to Galway	1h 55m
Dublin Heuston to Galway	2h 25m
Dublin Heuston to Tralee	3h 55m
Dublin Heuston to Westport	3h 10m
Dublin Heuston to Ballina	3h 15m
Dublin Connolly to Sligo	3h 15m
Dublin Connolly to Rosslare	3h

Northern Ireland

NI Railways' popular routes are:

Route	Travel time
Belfast Central to Dublin Connolly	2h 10m
Belfast to Bangor	31m
Belfast to Derry Londonderry	2h 05m
Belfast to Larne	50m
Belfast to Newry	57m

Portrush to Coleraine	12m

Reservations

Reservations for InterCity (IC) trains are optional in the Republic of Ireland. They may be purchased locally or online at www.irishrail.ie.

Northern Ireland
Train reservations are not necessary.

Additional information about rail travel in Ireland
Airport - station connections
Airlink buses run from Dublin airport to Heuston and Connolly train stations (bus 748). Eurail Passes are not usable on the bus.

The railway station at Sydenham is located near Belfast International Airport.

- Rail Travel Centre Connoly Station, Amiens Street, Dublin 1
  Mon-Sat: 7.00 - 22.20 Sun: 8.30 - 21.30
- At, NIR Travel Great Victoria Street Station, Belfast, BT2 7UB
  Mon-Fri: 9.00 - 17.00 Sat: 9.00 - 12.30

Ferry connections

Your Eurail Pass permits you to reduce ferry crossings to France and the United Kingdom from Irish Ferries, Norfolkline, and Stena Line.

Ireland Pass

- Make the most of your holiday by seeing Ireland by train.
- Standard pricing starts at $ 120.

Global Pass

- You are free to visit Ireland and up to 32 other European countries.
- Standard pricing begins at $ 211.

Ireland Tips and Techniques

Quick facts

- Capitals: Dublin (Republic of Ireland),
  Belfast (Northern Ireland).
- Population: 4.6 million, 1.9 million
- Language: English Irish
- currency: Euro (EUR), British Pound (GBP).
- Dialing code: +353, +44

In Ireland, names are spelled differently.

When trying to locate the correct rail station in Ireland, knowing the local spelling of cities comes in handy! Here are some locations to visit in Ireland:

- Corcaigh = Cork
- Gaillimh = Galway
- Cill = Kilkenny
- Cill Airne = Chainnigh Killarney
- Luimneach = Limerick.
- Mala = Mallow

The major rail stations in Ireland

Republic of Ireland

Dublin has two major rail stations. There is no rail connection between these stations, thus you must use a tram or bus to go from one to the other.

- Dublin Connolly
- Dublin Heuston

Northern Ireland
- Belfast Central

Discounts on Ferry tickets and other services
Use an Interrail Pass in Ireland to save 30% on ferry routes to England, France, Scotland, and Wales.
Guided train tours
- Get up to €30 off rail trips from Dublin.

Belgium

Despite its modest size, Belgium is packed with sights and activities. Visit the cosmopolitan city of Brussels and take the train to famous destinations such as Bruges, Ghent, and Antwerp. Visit the Ardennes area and sample some Belgian beers and wonderful chocolate along the route.

Routes Map

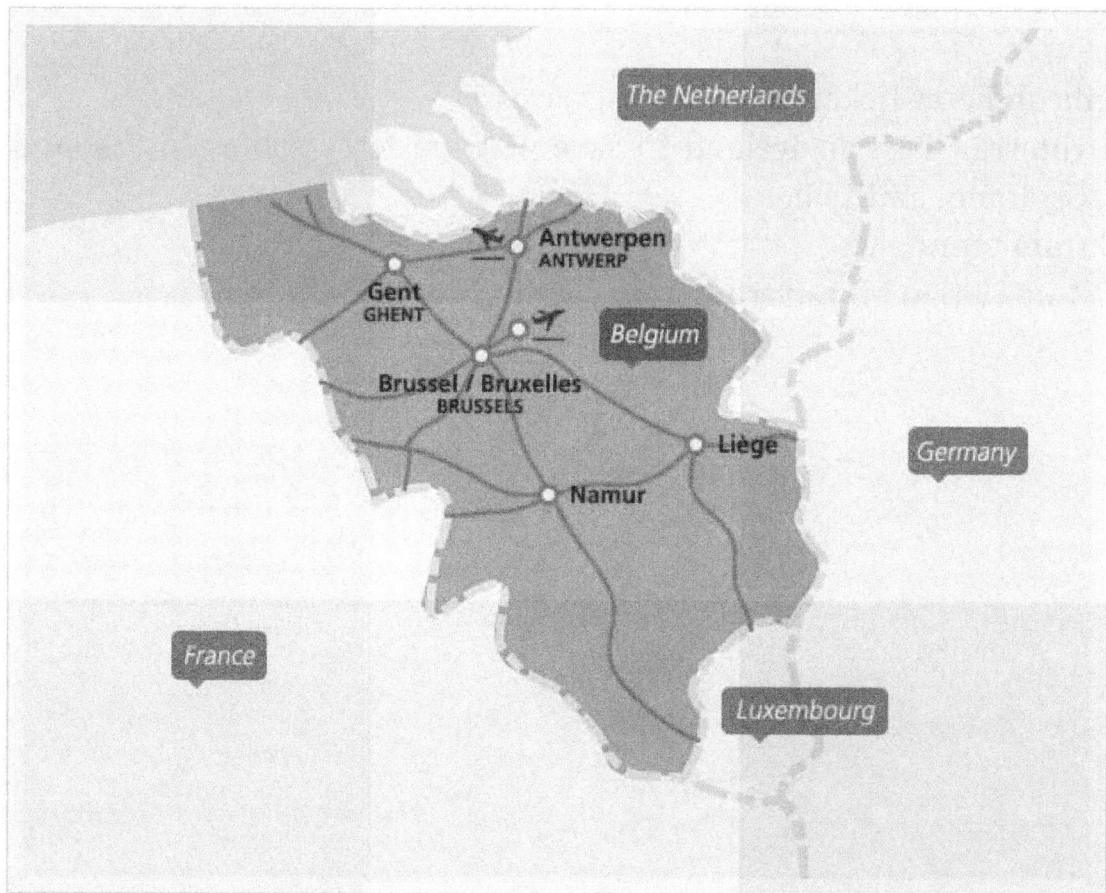

Belgium Train Types

Domestic Trains

In Belgium, there are many train kinds available to carry you. NMBS/SNCB operates the Belgian network. To check train times in Belgium, visit eurail.com.Regional and intercity trains in Belgium

InterCity trains (IC)

- connect bigger cities such as Brussels, Antwerp, and Liège.
- International trip to The Hague/Rotterdam (Netherlands), Luxembourg City, and Lille Flandres (France).
- There is no need for a reservation.

CityRail trains

- Run in the Brussels region.
- There is no need for a reservation.

Brussels Airport Express trains

- Runs from Brussels Airport to Antwerp, Ghent, and Brussels.
- A $5 supplement is needed.

International High-speed Trains in Belgium

Eurostar (ES)

- high-speed train service that connects United Kingdom, France, the Netherlands, and Germany on the routes.
  - Brussels - Lille - London
  - Amsterdam - Rotterdam - Antwerp - Brussels - Paris
  - Amsterdam - Rotterdam - Antwerp - Brussels - Disneyland Paris
  - Dortmund - Düsseldorf - Cologne - Liège - Brussels - Paris

Reservations are required for certain trains, which might be completely booked. I encourage you to make your bookings as soon as possible to prevent disappointment.

Former Thalys trains in red provide services to Amsterdam, Dortmund, and (Disney) Paris.

ICE

ICE trains travel from Brussels to Cologne and Frankfurt in Germany. Reservations are optional but advised since seats may fill up fast.

TGV

TGV trains travel from Brussels to many French locations, including Lille, Marne la Vallée Chessy (Disneyland), Strasbourg, Rennes, Nantes, Lyon, Marseille, and Montpellier.

Reservations are mandatory.

Other international trains in Belgium

ÖBB Nightjet
- Brussels - Nürnberg - Linz - Vienna
- Reservations must be made.

International IC
- Brussels - Namur - Luxembourg
- Brussels - Antwerp - Rotterdam - Amsterdam
- Antwerp - Gent - Kortrijk - Lille
- Liège - Luxembourg
- There are no reservation.

European Sleeper
- Brussels - Antwerp - Rotterdam -
  - Amsterdam - Berlin
- Reservations are required
- three times a week.

Popular connections

Domestic Connection

View estimated InterCity train travel times between prominent Belgian cities:

Route	Travel time
Brussels to Antwerp	47m
Brussels to Bruges	56m
Brussels to Ghent	31m
Brussels to Liège	58m
Ghent to Antwerp	55m

International Connection

Route	Which train?	Travel time	Reservations
Brussels to London (Great Britain)	Eurostar	3h	Required
Brussels to Luxembourg City (Luxembourg)	InterCity	3h	None
Brussels to Paris (France)	Eurostar	1h 30m	Required
Brussels to Amsterdam	InterCity	3h	None

(Netherlands)

Brussels to Marseille (France)	TGV	5h 30m	Required
Brussels to Vienna (Austria)	ÖBB Nightjet	14h 30m (overnight)	Required
Brussels to Berlin (Germany)	European Sleeper	11h 30m (overnight)	Required

Reservations

Eurail reservation self-service system
- Eurail
- Eurostar, TGV, ICE, RailJet, Nightjet

Booking via Eurail self-service in costly administrative fees.
- EUR 2,- per person per train
- Additional € 9,- per order (for paper tickets)

With railway carriers

- SNCB (b-europe): International trains to the Netherlands, France, and the United Kingdom
  - Eurostar and TGV (CDG and Disney only)
- DB (German Railways): International trains

- ICE

ÖBB (Austrian Railways): International trains

- ICE

CD (Czech railways): International trains

- ICE

European Sleeper: Only European Sleeper trains, international

Locally in Belgium, at the rail station

Eurostar trains are popular and, as a result, they frequently sell out rapidly. Make sure you obtain your seat reservation in advance. Alternatively, you may select trains without seat reservations in the timetable by clicking the 'no reservation required' option.

Belgium Pass

- Discover Belgium, the Netherlands, and Luxembourg by train.
- Prices start at $ 118

Global Pass

- Have the flexibility to explore Belgium and up to 30 additional European countries.
- Standard pricing begins at $ 211.

Belgium Tips and Techniques

Quick Facts

- Capital: Brussels
- Population of 11 million people.
- Languages: Dutch (Flemish), French, and German
- Currency: Euro (EUR)
- Dialing code: +32

Belgium's Train Stations

The major hub stations in Belgium are Bruxelles Midi/Brussel Zuid, Brussel Centraal, Brussel Noord, Antwerpen Centraal, Gent Sint-Pieters, and Luik Guillemins. Trains to Belgium's major cities and numerous overseas destinations may be connected at these rail stations.

Station Facilities

Stations in Belgium often offer good amenities, which generally include:

- Luggage lockers
- Foreign exchange desks
- Restaurants and cafés
- ATM cash machines in tourist information offices
- Elevators and escalators
- Access for travelers with disabilities

The spelling of city names

The local spelling of Belgian towns and train stations is commonly seen on the Eurail train schedule and at stations.

Here is the local spelling of several well-known Belgian cities:

- Antwerp = Antwerpen
- Bruges = Brugge

- Brussels = Brussel/Bruxelles
- Ghent = Gent
- Ostend = Oostende

Transportation and lodging packages

With a valid Eurail Pass in Belgium, you may travel by bus to adjacent countries and get a 10% discount at the Brussels Meininger Hotel.

Bosnia-Herzegovina

Bosnia & Herzegovina, which is progressively becoming a famous tourist destination, has an extraordinary mix of history and natural scenery. Explore Sarajevo's unique capital city, go white-water rafting, and visit the spectacular Kravica waterfalls with your Eurail Pass.

Routes Map

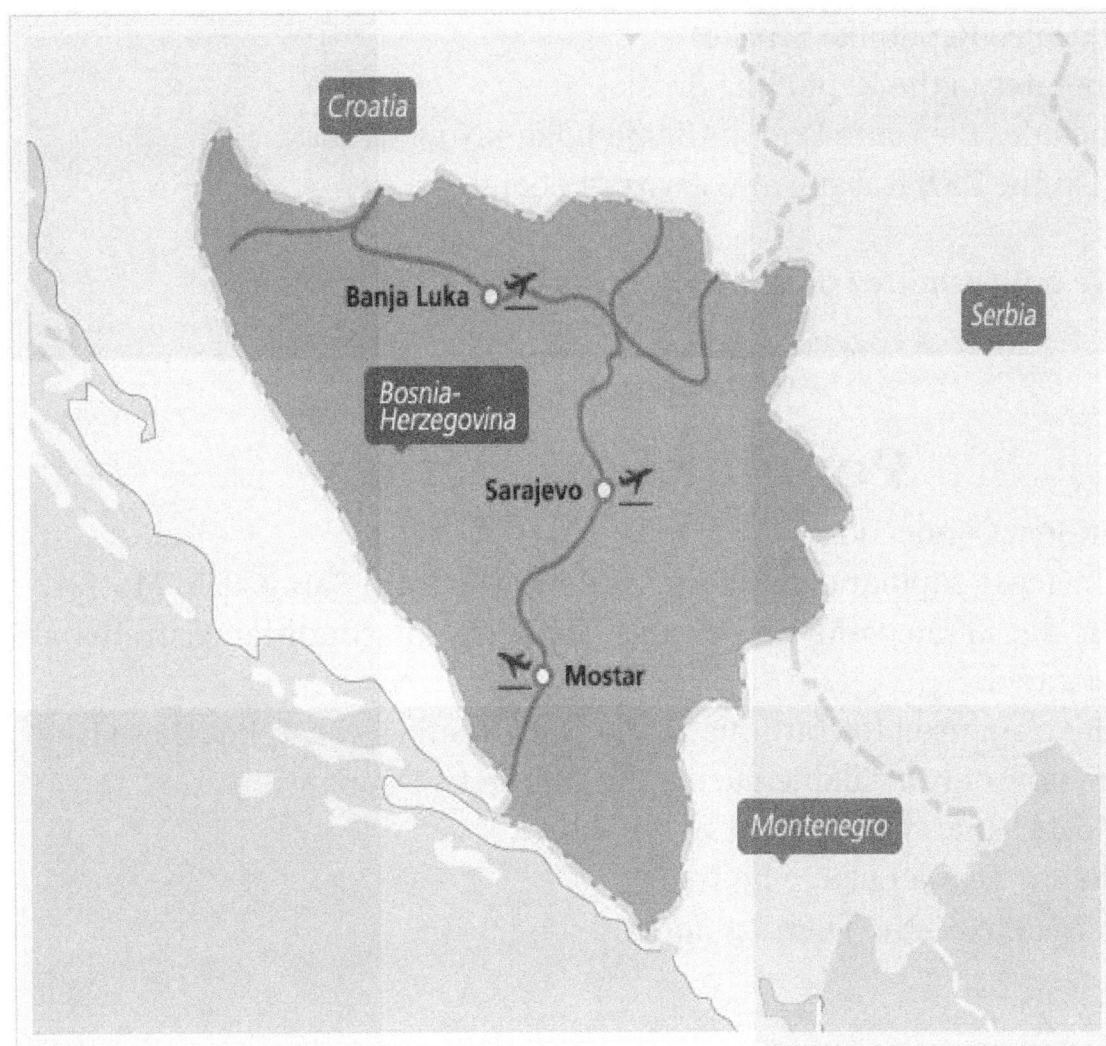

Train Types

Domestic trains

Two railway companies operate in various parts of Bosnia and Herzegovina.

ZFBH (eljeznice Federacije Bosne i Hercegovine)
- operates in the Federation of Bosnia and Herzegovina.
- Includes the major route Doboj - Sarajevo - Mostar - Ploe.
- Visit the English version of the ZFBH website at www.zfbh.ba/en/.

ZRS (eljeznice Republike Srpske)
- operates in the Republika Srpska.
- Includes the route Doboj - Banja Luka - Novi Grad.
- Visit the ZRS website at www.zrs-rs.com

Bikes are not permitted on trains in Bosnia and Herzegovina.

Popular Connection

International Connection
- The most popular and picturesque route is from Sarajevo to Mostar.
- On the Sarajevo-Mostar routes, modern, air-conditioned trains are operated.
- The train used to continue to Ploe on Croatia's coast, but these trains are now only available during the summer season.
- Mostar - Sarajevo: 2 hours
- Doboj - Banja Luka: 2 hours
- Banja Luka - Novi Grad 2 hours

Reservations

Train bookings in Bosnia and Herzegovina:

Reservations for regional trains are required. You may reserve your seat at the train station.

- The reservation charge is €1.50 (BAM 3, the local currency).
- The cost of the reservation is determined by the distance traveled.

Bosnia - Herzegovina Pass

Global Pass

- Have the flexibility to explore Bosnia and Herzegovina as well as up to 32 other European countries.
- Standard pricing begins at $ 211.

Bosnia - Herzegovina Travel Tips

Quick Facts

- Population: 4.5 million
- Languages: Bosnian, Croatian, and Serbian
- Currency: Bosnia and Herzegovina Convertible Mark (BAM)
- Dialing code: +387

Bulgaria

Bulgaria has nearly 4000 kilometers of rail track. The primary rail hub is in Sofia, the capital city, which has links to Romania, Serbia, and Turkey. On board Bulgarian trains, you may enjoy a variety of magnificent landscapes. Bulgaria has an interesting historical and cultural history, as well as beautiful scenery. Visit Sofia, which is set in the foothills of two mountains and packed with interesting views and noise. Your Eurail Bulgaria Pass is your passport to a fantastic rail trip.

Routes Map

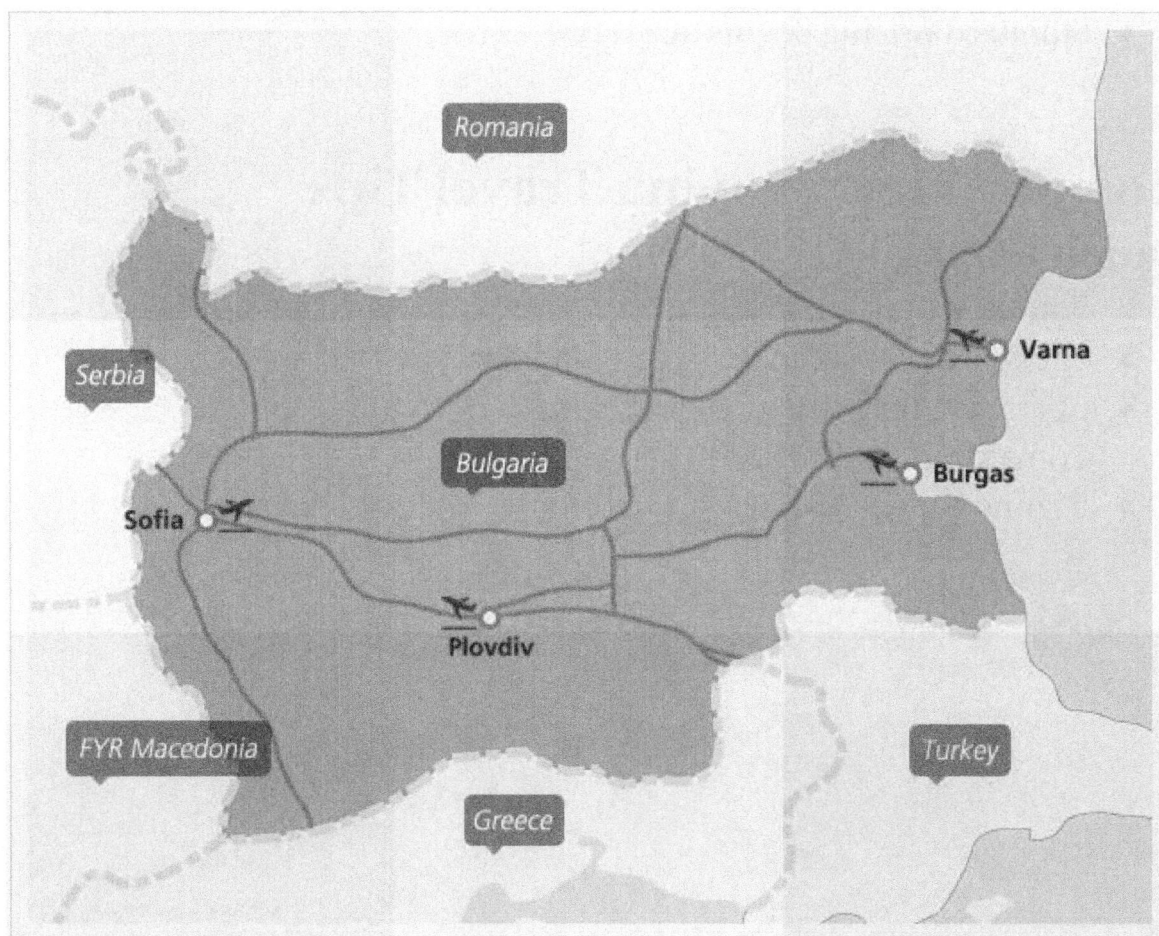

Train types

Bulgarian State Railways (BDZ) operates the country's rail network. Train timetables may be found on the Eurail website at eurail.com or on the BDZ website at www.bdz.bg/en

Domestic trains in Bulgaria

Expresen Vlak
- Faster trains
- Sofia to Plovdiv, Varna, Burgas, and Ruse
- Reservations are necessary (about €0.25, or BGN 0.50 in local currency).

Barz Vlak
- Local 'fast' trains.
- There is no need for a reservation.

Patnicheski
- Slower local trains.
- There is no need for a reservation.

Rhodope Scenic Railway
- Septemvri - Dobrinishte
- Narrow gauge trains

In Bulgaria, you may carry your bike on the train. The price is 2 BGN (Bulgarian lev, about €1) and may be paid at the ticket counter.

International Trains in Bulgaria

Presently, the only international daylight connections are to and from Romania. Connections between Serbia and Greece are presently halted due to construction and operational concerns.
- Sofia - Ruse - Bucharest

- From June 21st until October 9th, solely from Sofia.
- Between October and June, this train only travels from Ruse to Bucharest.
- Reservations must be made.

- Varna - Ruse - Bucharest
  - From June 21st until October 9th, Runs from Varna.
  - Between October and June, this train only travels from Ruse to Bucharest.
  - Reservations must be made.

- (Istanbul -) Dimitrovgrad - Veliko Tarnovo - Ruse - Bucharest
  - Only runs from June 21st to October 9th from Istanbul.
  - Between October and June, this train only travels from Ruse to Bucharest.
  - Reservations must be made.
- Vidin - Craiova
- No reservations are required for local trains.

Domestic night trains in Bulgaria

Bulgaria has a variety of domestic night trains, all of which go from Sofia to the east. During the summer, trains to the Black Sea coast towns of Varna and Burgas are very popular.

- Sofia - Plovdiv - Varna
  - Seats and sleepers
- Sofia - Pleven - Varna
  - Seats and sleepers
- Sofia - Karlovo - Varna
  - Seats and sleepers
- Sofia - Plovdiv - Burgas
  - Seats and sleepers
- Sofia - Karlovo - Burgas
  - Seats and sleepers
- Sofia - Pleven - Ruse - Silistra
  - Seats and couchettes

International night trains in Bulgaria

Currently, the sole international night train in Bulgaria links Sofia and Plovdiv to Istanbul, Turkey. Make sure to book several days ahead of time, particularly in the summer. This train may only be reserved at rail stations.

- Sofia - Plovdiv - Istanbul Halkali
  - Runs All year round
  - Modern Turkish couchette and sleeping cars
  - Reservations must be made.
- Bucharest - Ruse - Veliko Tarnovo -
  - Dimitrovgrad - Istanbul Halkali
  - Only from June 21st to October 9th from Varna.
  - Modern Turkish couchette and sleeping vehicles
  - Reservations must be made.

Population Connection

Reservations are not required for the following train lines in Bulgaria:

Route	Travel time
Sofia to Varna	7h 30m
Sofia to Burgas	5h 30m

Sofia to Plovdiv	2h 30m
Sofia to Vidin	5h
Sofia to Ruse	6h 5m
Plovdiv to Burgas	3h 50m

International Routes

Sofia offers direct international rail connections to a number of countries. Reservations are advised.

Route	Which train?	Travel time	Reservations
Sofia to Bucharest (Romania)	International (INT 460)	10h 50m	Required

Ruse to Bucharest (Romania)	Intercity (INT 460)	2h 50m	Required
Vidin to Craiova (Romania)	Regional	3h 50m	No
Sofia to Istanbul (Turkey)*	International (INT)	13h	Optional

*The train from Sofia to Istanbul ends at Istanbul Halkali station, from whence you may catch a metro/Marmaray train to the city center and beneath the Bosphorus to the Asian side. Make sure you have Turkish Lira notes on hand since most metro ticket machines do not accept bank cards.

Reservations

It is not possible to make a reservation using the Eurail reservation self-service system.
 Locally in Bulgaria, at the rail station

How can I book rail tickets in Bulgaria?
- Local ticket counters at rail stations
- At Rila travel agencies, which may be found at rail stations around Bulgaria.
- Check out the BDZ website at www.bdz.bg/en for locations.
- A reservation is known as "zapazeno myasto" in Bulgarian.

Bulgaria Pass

- Use your whole holiday to explore Bulgaria by train.
- Standard pricing begins at $ 59.

Global Pass

- You are free to visit Bulgaria and up to 32 other European countries.
- Standard pricing begins at $ 211.

Bulgaria Tips & Tricks

Quick Facts

- Sofia (spelled Sofiya, written as София) is the capital.
- Population: 7.3 million
- Language: Bulgarian
- Currency: Bulgarian Lev (BGN)
- Dialing code: +359

Airport - station connection

Buses (lines 84 and 284) go from Sofia Airport to the main train station. Eurail passes are not usable on the bus.

Bulgarian Eurail help office

If you have questions concerning Eurail, go to the international ticket office at Sofia train station. More help offices throughout Europe can be found on the website Eurail aid offices.

Bulgarian city spelling

The local spelling of Bulgarian towns and stations is commonly used on Bulgarian rail schedules and at train stations in Bulgaria.

Here is the local spelling of several well-known Bulgarian cities:

- Sofiya = Sofia

Czech Republic

Your Eurail Czech Republic Pass will get you access to a real rail trip. The allure of Prague (Praha) is well-recognized across the globe, and the whole nation will wow you with its rich history and stunning natural beauty. Step aboard and see what awaits you on your Czech rail excursion.

Routes Map

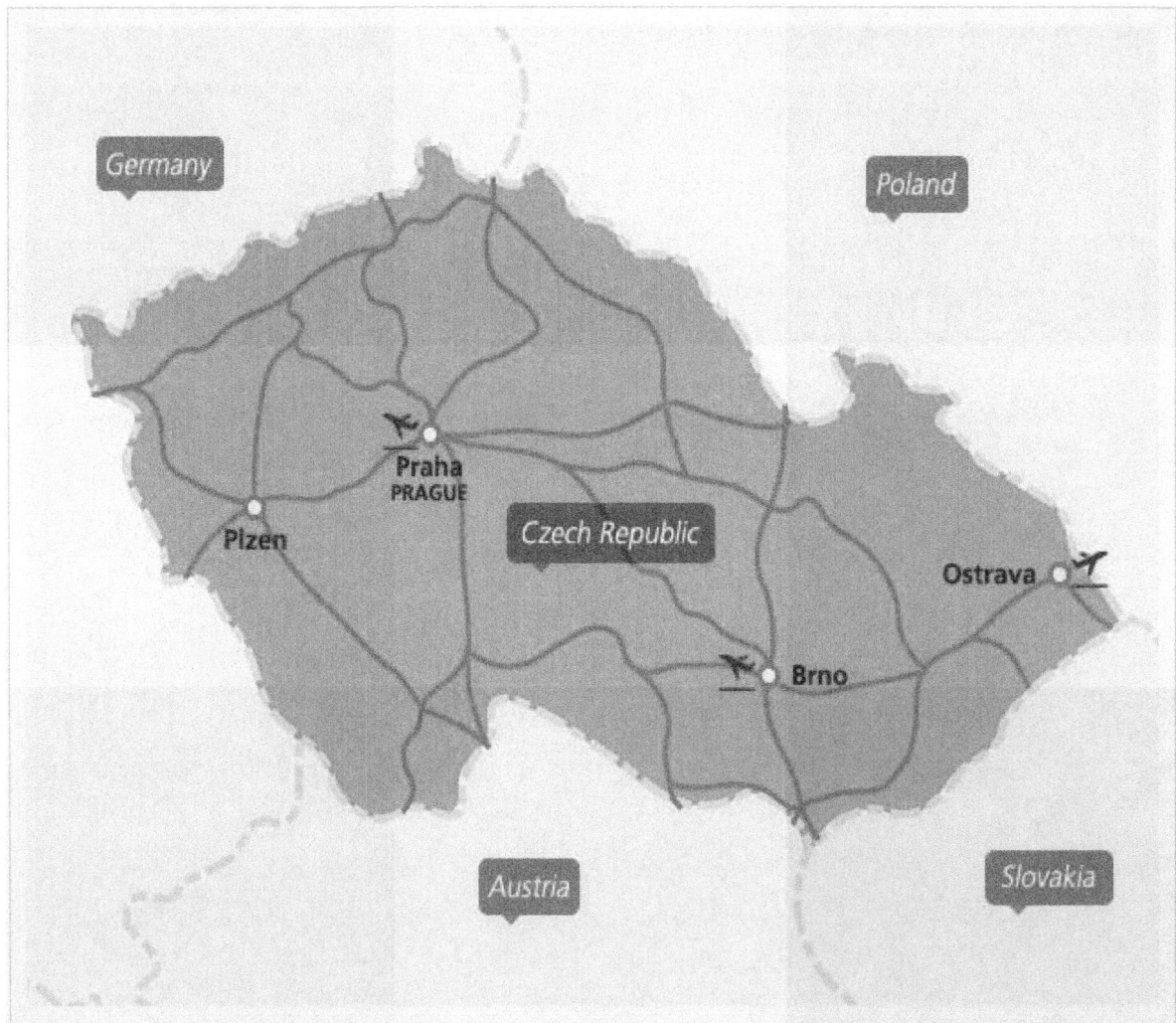

Train Types

Regional trains in the Czech Republic are operated by the Czech national railroads, eské dráhy. International trains go to and from the Czech Republic.

Train timings in the Czech Republic can be seen on the Eurail timetable at eurail.com.

Domestic Trains in the Czech Republic

Osobni
- Commuter trains

Spěšný (Sp)
- Special inter-regional trains

Rychllk (R)
- Inter-regional trains

Expres (Ex)
- Regional trains stop exclusively at certain stops.

SC SuperCity
- Trains that travel at high speeds between large cities
- Reservations are necessary.

InterCity (IC)
- Trains run between bigger cities.
- Reservations are needed for certain IC trains.

Eurocity (EC)
- Trains run between major cities.
- Reservations are advised.

Bikes are permitted on most trains in the Czech Republic. A bike ticket must be purchased in advance.

International Czech Railways

International trains travel from the Czech Republic to Slovakia, Poland, Germany, Hungary, Austria, and Switzerland:

Eurocity (EC)
- Prague - Brno - Bratislava - Budapest
- Prague - Dresden - Berlin (- Hamburg)
- Prague - Ceske Budejovice - Linz
- Prague - Plzen - Regensburg - Munich
- Prague - Pardubice - Ostrava - Katowice - Warsaw
- Prague - Pardubice - Ostrava - Katowice - Krakow - Przemysl
- (Graz -) Breclav - Ostrava - Katowice - Krakow - Przemysl

RailJet (RJ)
- Prague - Pardubice - Brno
  - Vienna - Graz

SuperCity (SC)
- Prague - Ostrava - Zilina -
  Poprad - Kosice

InterCity (IC)
- Prague - Ostrava - Zilina -
  - Poprad - Kosice

LEO Express
International train connects the Czech Republic, Slovakia, and Poland. This train requires an Interrail Global Pass or a Czech Republic Pass to board. Reservations are free, however, they must be made before boarding.

Tickets may be reserved up to three months in advance on the website www.leoexpress.com/en or at ticket offices in Prague, Olomouc, and Ostrava-Svinov.

Routes available:

- Prague - Pardubice - Olomouc - Prerov - Staré Msto
- Prague - Pardubice - Olomouc - Prerov - Ostrava - Bohumin - Zilina - Poprad - Kosice
- Prague - Pardubice - Olomouc - Prerov - Ostrava - Katowice - Krakow
- Prerov - Hulin - Otrokovice - Staré Mesto
- (Prague -) Usti and Orlici - Letohrad - Lichkov - Kraliky - Moravsky Karlov

RegioJet

- International trains travel between the Czech Republic, Poland, Slovakia, Austria, and Hungary. This train requires an Interrail Global Pass or a Czech Republic Pass to board.
- Most trains need reservations.
- Tickets may be purchased up to three months in advance on the regiojet.com website.
- Reservations are required on the following (RJ) routes:
  - Prague - Pardubice - Olomouc - Ostrava - Kosice (night train)
  - Prague - Pardubice - Olomouc - Ostrava - Krakow - Przemysl (night train)
  - Prague - Pardubice - Olomouc - Ostrava - Opava/Bohumin/ /Havirov/Navsi
  - Prague - Pardubice - Olomouc - Ostrava - Havirov - Zilina - Poprad - Kosice
  - Prague - Brno - Bratislava (- Zilina)

- Prague - Brno - Vienna
- Prague - Brno - Vienna -
  Gyor - Budapest
- Ostrava - Krakow (bus route)
- Reservations are not required on the following (R) routes:
  - Brno - Perov - Ostrava - Bohumn
  - Koln - St nad Labem (valid on R23).
- Seasonal direct trains from Prague to Rijeka are not always included.
  (RJ 1044/1047/1367/1364)

Night Trains

Night trains travel from the Czech Republic to Slovakia, Poland, Germany, Hungary, Austria, and Switzerland:

Euro Night (EN)
- Prague - Dresden - Leipzig - Frankfurt - Basel - Zurich
- Prague - Ceske Budejovice -
  - Linz - Zurich
- Prague - Brno - Breclav -
  - Bratislava - Budapest
- Prague - Pardubice - Ostrava - Kosice
- Prague - Pardubice - Ostrava - Kosice - Humenne
- Prague - Pardubice - Ostrava - Krakow - Warsaw
- Graz/Budapest - Breclav -
  - Ostrava - Krakow - Warsaw

Deutsche Bahn operates a sitting carriage on the route Prague-Leipzig-Zurich under EC number 459/458. Reservations for this carriage are not required.

ÖBB Nightjet (NJ)
- Graz/Budapest - Breclav -
  -Ostrava - Wroclaw - Berlin

RegioJet (RJ)

- Prague - Pardubice - Olomouc - Ostrava - Zilina - Poprad - Kosice
- Prague - Pardubice - Olomouc - Ostrava - Krakow - Przemysl

Popular connections

Domestic Connection

Average train travel times between major cities in the Czech Republic are;

Route	Travel time
Prague to Brno	2h 30m
Prague to Olomouc	2h 30m
Prague to Ostrava	3h 30m
Prague to Pilsen (Plzeň)	1h 30m

International Connection

Route	Which train?	Travel time	Reservations
Prague to Berlin (Germany)	EuroCity	4h 30m	Optional
Prague to Bratislava (Slovakia)	EuroCity / RegioJet	4h	Required (EuroCity) / Optional (RegioJet)
Prague to Budapest (Hungary)	EuroCity	7h	Optional
Prague to Vienna	Railjet /	4h	Optional

(Austria)	RegioJet		
Prague to Warsaw (Poland)	EuroCity	8h	Required

Reservations

Reservation system for Eurail
- Eurail

Administration fees when booking through Eurail self-service
- € 2,- per person per train
- Additional € 9,- per order (for paper tickets)

With railway carriers
- **CD (Czech railways):** Domestic and international trains
- **Leo Express:** Only Leo Express trains, both domestic and international.
- **RegioJet:** Only RegioJet trains, both domestic and international.
- **ÖBB (Austrian Railways):** Domestic and international trains

Locally in the Czech Republic, at the train station

Czech Republic Pass

- Use your vacation to explore the Czech Republic by train.
- Standard prices start at $ 92.

Global Pass

- Explore the Czech Republic and up to 32 other European countries.
- Standard pricing begins at $ 211.

Czech Republic Tips and tricks

Quick Facts

- Prague (local spelling: Praha) is the capital.
- Population: 10.5 million
- Language: Czech
- Czech Koruna (CZK)
- Dialing code: +420

Czech cities' spellings

The local spelling of Czech cities and stations can usually be found on Czech train timetables and at Czech train stations.

Here is the local spelling of some well-known Czech cities:

Praha = Prague

Plze = Pilsen

Link between the airport and the station

There are bus connections to Prague's public transportation system as well as the Airport Express Bus to Prague's main station from the airport. Note: Eurail Passes are not valid on the bus.

Czech Republic's Eurail help office

If you have any questions about Eurail, go to the international ticket office at Prague Liben station (Praha Liben). It is open daily from 06.00 to 20.50.

Main train stations in the Czech Republic

Prague is the main railway hub. The most important train stations are: Hlavn nádraz (Main Station). The largest station. It has ticket offices, a train information center, and a Prague information service.

Nádraz Holesovice (Holesovice Station). Trains from Berlin and other northern destinations usually terminate here.

Both are served by the city's metro line C.

Denmark

Your Eurail Pass is your passport to everything Danish. When traveling by rail in Denmark, you'll find everything you're searching for, whether it's dynamic towns, attractive beaches, lush forests, or breathtaking countryside. And your Eurail pass will get you there fast and easily.

Routes Map

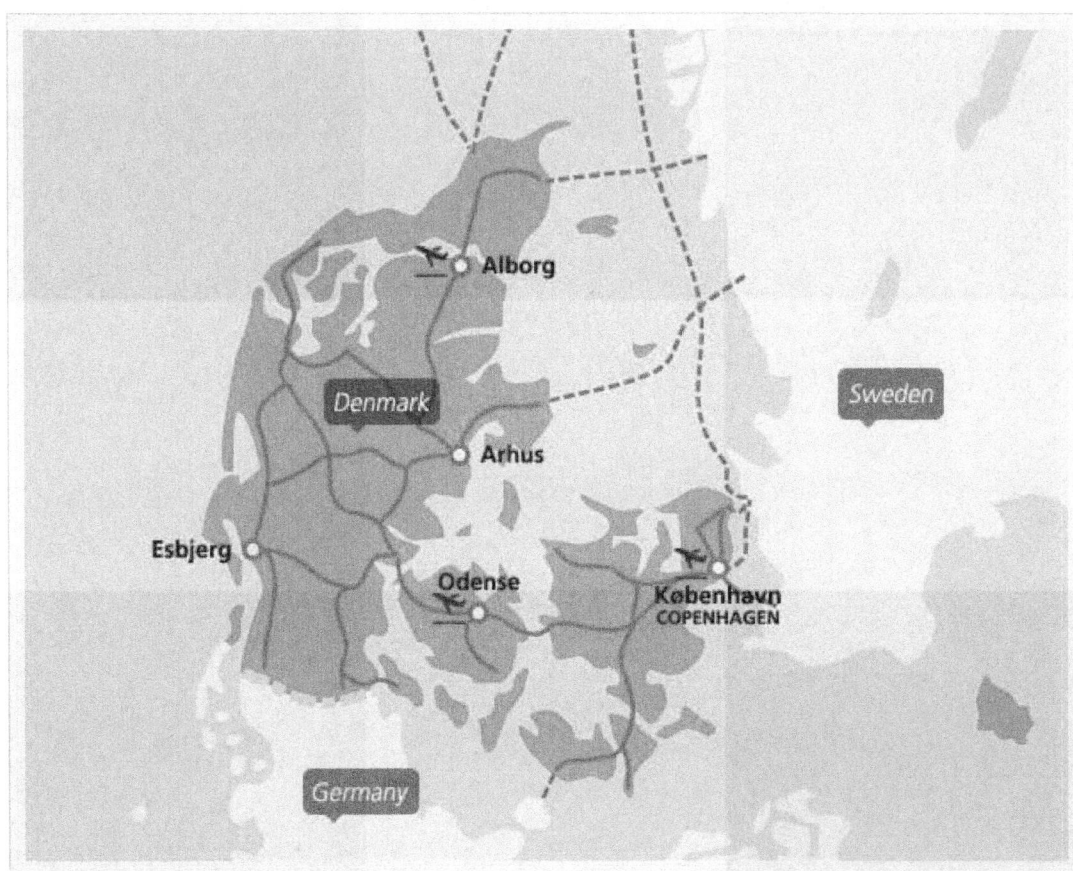

Train types

Domestic Trains

Denmark's national railway corporation is named DSB (Danish State Railways - Danske Statsbaner).

Valid Eurail Passes in Denmark are also valid on trains operated by the following railway companies:

Arriva, DSB S-Tog, and DSBFirst.

Regional trains (RØ, RV, ØR, IR)

- Regional trains run across Denmark.

InterCity and InterCity Lyn (IC, ICL)

- Faster than regional trains
- Various roads in Denmark

S-Tog

- Suburban Trains in Copenhagen are fully covered in your Interrail Pass.

Nordjyske Jernbaner (NJ)

- fully included in your Interrail Pass.

Lokaltog (RE)

- Sjaelland's local trains
- Fully included in the pass

Private railway companies in Denmark

- The majority are covered by your Interrail Pass.

Bicycles are allowed on the train with the purchase of a specific bike ticket. From May to August, bike spaces on IC and ICL trains must be reserved in advance.

International Trains

SJ High-speed train
- from Copenhagen to Stockholm (Sweden)

InterCity Express (ICE)
- Copenhagen - Hamburg
- Aarhus - Hamburg

Reservations fare required during the summer months (17 June to 21 August 2023).

Snälltget
- Copenhagen restad - Stockholm (Night train from Berlin and Hamburg)

SJ Euronight (EN)
- Berlin (from 31 March) - Hamburg -
  - Copenhagen Airport - Malmö - Stockholm
- Runs every day.

Snälltåget
- Berlin - Hamburg - Copenhagen
  - Malmö - Stockholm
- Every day except Saturdays.

Also runs as a day train from Copenhagen Restad to Stockholm.

Popular connections

Domestic

The following are the average travel times between Denmark's major cities. Seat reservations are not required for any of these train journeys.

Route	Travel time
Copenhagen to Alborg	4h 45m
Copenhagen to Arhus	3h 20m
Copenhagen to Esbjerg	3h 35m
Copenhagen to Odense	1h 45m
Aalborg to Hirtshals (ferry to Norway)	1h 05m

Aalborg to Frederikshavn

1h 10m

(Ferry to Norway and Sweden)

Reservations

How can I book rail tickets in Denmark?
Reservation system for Eurail
- Eurail
- Administration costs when booking via Eurail self-service
- EUR 2,- per person per train
- Additional € 9,- per order (for paper tickets)

With railway carriers
- DSB (Danish Railways): Domestic trains IC, IC-Lyn DSB (via b-europe): Domestic and international trains excluding Sweden
- SJ (Swedish Railways): International trains to/from Sweden only X2000, EN Snälltaget Berlin - Stockholm: Only Berlin - Copenhagen - Stockholm night train
- DB (German Railways): International trains to Germany IC

locally at the train station

Which trains in Denmark need reservations?
- Intercity (IC trains to and from Germany): €4,50 (DKK 33) in 2nd class and €5,90 (DKK 44) in 1st class. Only required for the summer season (17 June to 21 August)

- SJ Euronight: costs vary depending on location and kind of seat/bed booked.

- Snälltget: costs vary depending on the location and kind of seat/bed reserved.

Reservations are essential for lengthy travels.
InterCity (IC) and InterCityLyn (ICL): roughly €4 (DKK 30).

Denmark Pass

- Use your whole holiday to travel by train around Denmark.
- Standard pricing starts at $ 120.

Global Pass

- You are free to tour Denmark and up to 32 other European countries.
- Standard pricing begins at $ 211.

Scandinavia Pass

- Travel by rail across Finland, Denmark, Sweden, and Norway.
- Standard pricing starts at $ 190.

Denmark Tips and Techniques

Quick Facts

- Capital: Copenhagen (Kbenhavn).
- Population: 5.6 million
- Language: Danish

- Currency: Danish krone (DKK)
- dialing code: +45

Denmark city spelling

On Danish rail schedules and at Danish train stations, you'll normally discover the local spelling of Danish cities and stations.

Here is the local spelling of several well-known Danish cities:
- Copenhagen = Kbenhavn
- Denmark's Eurail help office

If you have any questions concerning Eurail, you may visit the international ticket counter at Central Station Kobenhavn (Copenhagen). It is opens daily from 9:30 a.m. until 6:00 p.m.

Airport-station link

Terminal 3 at Copenhagen Kastrup Airport contains a rail station. There are connections to Kobenhavn H (the main rail station in Copenhagen), Malmö (Sweden), and many more locations.

General rail travel information

For general information on rail travel in Denmark, contact the DSB Customer Centre: +45 70 13 14 15 (daily 08:00 - 20:00, English-speaking staff) or salginfo@dsb.dk.

Finland

Traveling by rail in Finland is a must for nature enthusiasts. Vast expanses of unspoiled natural landscape, including forests, lakes, and islands, are interrupted only by gorgeous towns and vibrant cities, such as Helsinki. Travel all the way north to Kolari, far beyond the Arctic Circle, to get a glimpse of the beautiful Northern Lights.

Routes Map

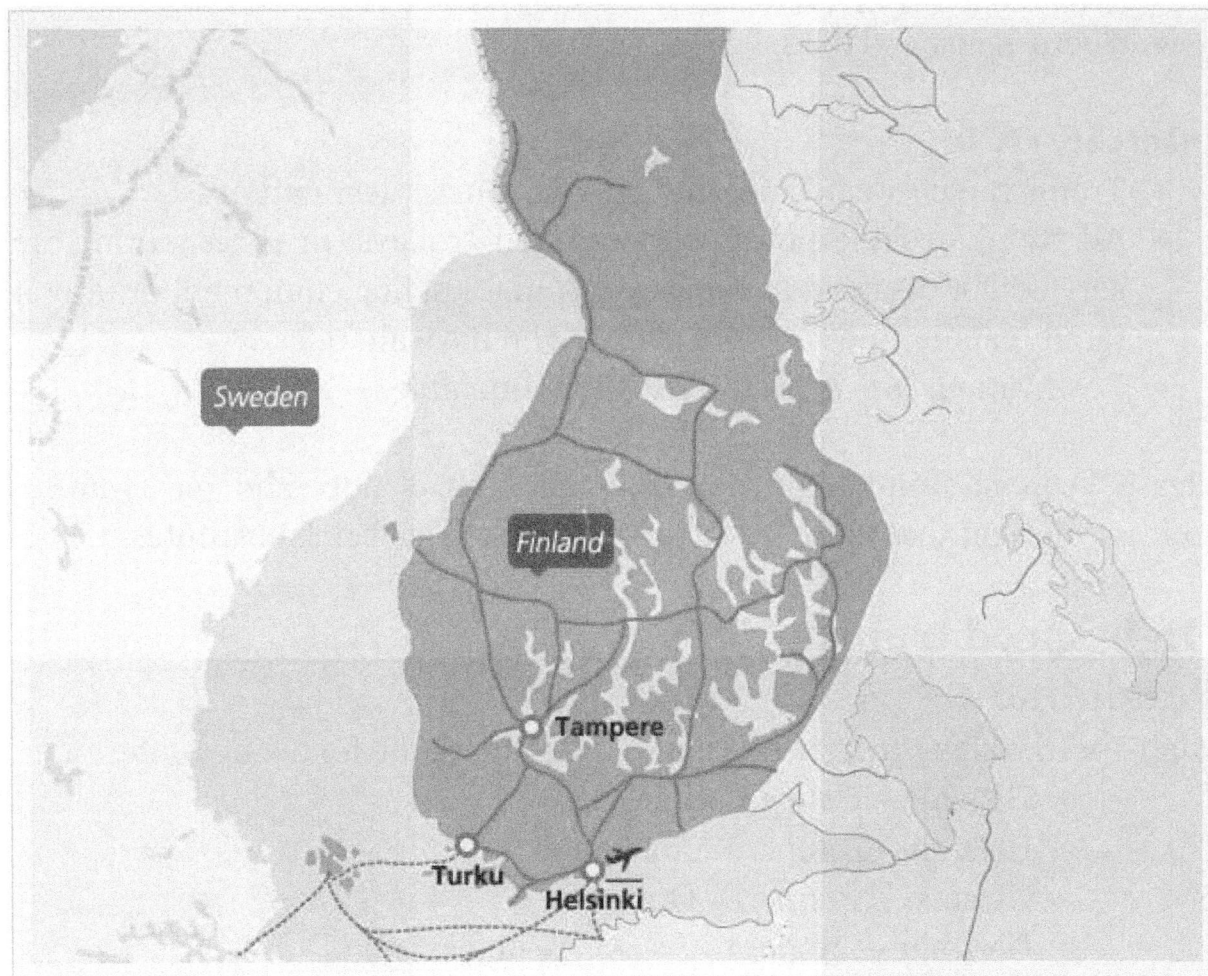

Types of Trains in Finland

VR operates Finland's passenger rail network. Finnish trains are modern and well-equipped. To check train timings in Finland, check the Eurail timetable.

Regional and intercity trains
Express train

- Interregional trains that travel great distances in southern Finland.
- All trains include power outlets, a restaurant car, and amenities for disabled passengers.
- There is no need to make reservations.

InterCity (IC)

- Trains run between cities and famous tourist destinations.
- All trains provide power outlets, food trolleys, or a restaurant car, services for disabled passengers, room for skiing equipment or prams, family cabins, and seats for people who have allergies.
- Reservations are advised. Check the timetable.

Please keep in mind that your Interrail Pass is not valid on TrainBus connections and that these buses are not utilized as train substitutes.

High-speed trains
Pendolino

High-speed trains run between major cities along the following routes:
- Helsinki - Tampere - Vaasa
- Helsinki - Tampere - Kokkola
- Helsinki - Tampere - Oulu
- Helsinki - Tampere - Jyväskylä - Pieksämäki
- Helsinki - Lahti - Kouvola - Kuopio - Kajaani - Oulu
- Helsinki - Lahti - Kouvola - Joensuu
- Helsinki - Tampere - Oulu

- All trains provide power outlets, WiFi, a restaurant car, services for disabled passengers, and seats for passengers with allergies.
- Reservations are advised.

Night Trains in Finland

Santa Claus Express offers numerous overnight alternatives that will take you around Finland. Night trains contain sleeping carriages as well as restaurant cars. Reservations are necessary.

- Helsinki - Rovaniemi
- Kemijärvi - Helsinki
- Helsinki - Kolari
- Turku - Rovaniemi

Popular connections

DOMESTIC ROUTES INTERNATIONAL FERRY ROUTES

Route	Travel time
Helsinki to Tampere	1h 30m
Helsinki to Turku	2h
Tampere to Turku	1h 45m

Helsinki to Oulu	6h / 9h (overnight)
Helsinki to Rovaniemi	8h 20m / 11h 50m (overnight)

International Routes

There are no direct rail connections between Finland and its neighbors, although there are international ferry links to Germany, Sweden, and Estonia.

Your Eurail Pass gives you discounts on ferry routes operated by Finnlines Ferries, Tallink Silja Lines, and Viking Lines:

- Helsinki to Stockholm (Sweden).
- Helsinki to Tallinn (Estonia)
- Helsinki to Travemünde (Lübeck, Germany).
- Turku to Stockholm (Sweden)

Reservations

How can I book rail tickets in Finland?

It is not possible to make a reservation using the Eurail reservation self-service system.

Call the VR (Finnish Railways) call center

- at +35 8 9 2319 2902. (open every day from 7 a.m. to 10 p.m. local time)

- VR is Finland's national railway corporation, and the staff speak English. You may make reservations over the phone (with a credit card) and pick them up at ticket machines at Finnish railway stations. You will get an email with a booking code. Reservations cannot be sent to your address. Skype may be used to contact the VR call center. This contact center can make bookings for Finnish high-speed and night trains.

locally at the train station

Reservations train costs in Finland

Intercity and Pendolino train

- Reservations for these trains are strongly advised.
- Seat reservations at VR cost 25% of the whole fee.
- All rates are subject to availability and vary by route:
  - Seat: €2,70 - €23,30

Sleeper trains (Santa Claus Express)

- These trains need reservations.
- VR presently only offers sleeping cabins as a whole, not as individual beds.
- Night train bookings at VR cost half the price of a full-fare ticket.
- All rates are subject to availability and vary by route:
  - Seat: €5 - €32,70
  - Double sleeper Cabins: €39 to €150.
  - Deluxe double sleeping cabin with private bathroom: €39 - €160

It is best to book early, particularly if you intend to go during the winter peak season. You will save money on reservation fees this way.

Finland Pass

- Use your whole holiday to travel by train around Finland.
- Standard fares start at $ 120.

Global Pass

- Feel free to visit Finland and up to 32 additional European countries.
- Standard fares start at $ 211.

Scandinavia Pass

- Travel by rail across Finland, Denmark, Sweden, and Norway.
- Standard rates begin at $ 190.

Finland Tips and Techniques

Quick Facts

- Helsinki is the capital city.
- Population: 5.4 million
- Languages: Finnish and Swedish
- Currency: Euro (EUR)
- dialing code: +358

Finland has a Eurail assistance office.
Visit the international ticket counter at Helsinki Central Station if you have any inquiries concerning Eurail. It is open from 10 a.m. to 5 p.m. Monday through Friday.

Link between the airport and the station
Commuter trains I and P offer regular connections from Helsinki Airport (Helsinki Lentoasema) to Helsinki City. Because these trains are run by VR, your Eurail pass is valid for this journey.

Estonia

It's time to go to northern Europe! Travel across Estonia with a Eurail Pass and experience the capital Tallinn, the outstanding history, and the wonderful national parks.

Routes Map

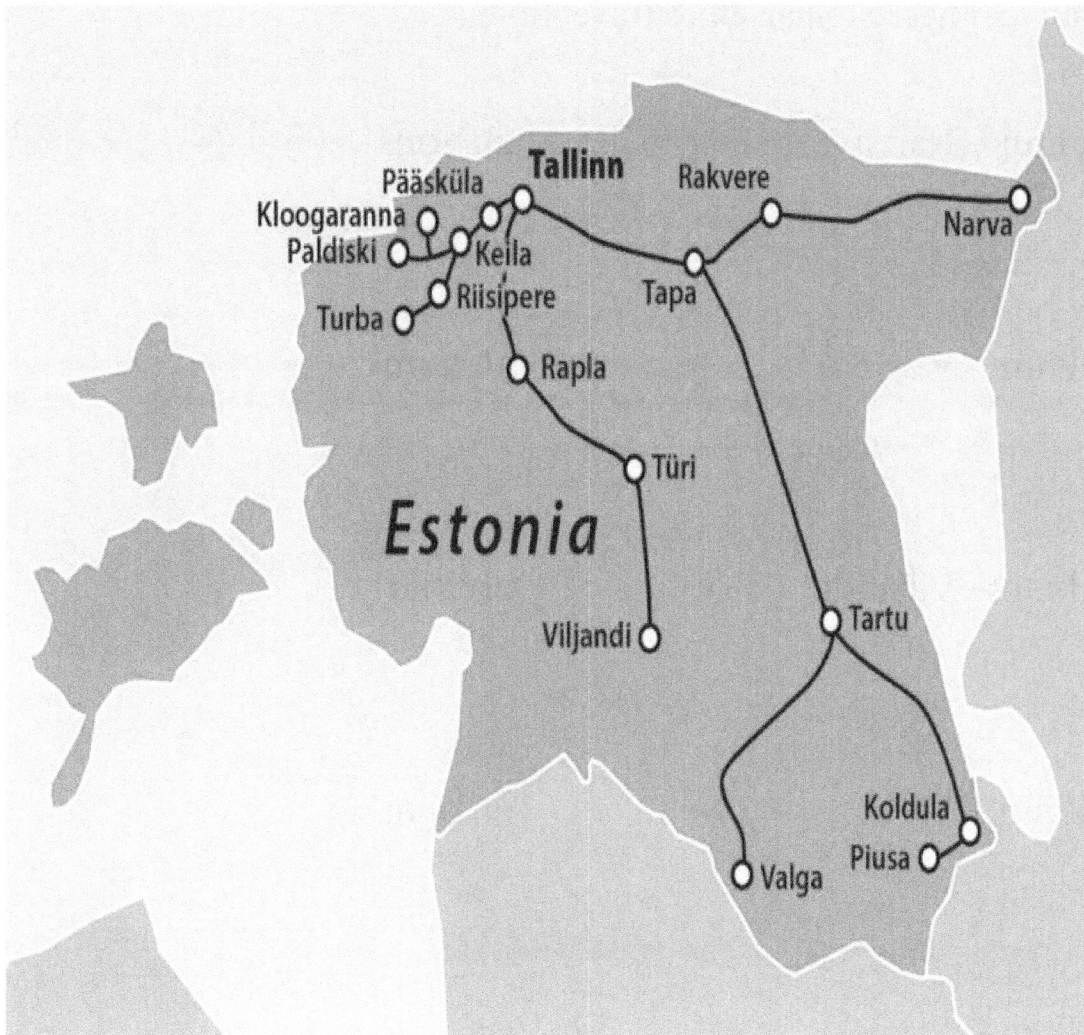

Train types in Estonia

Domestic rail services in Estonia are provided by Elron; see elron.ee/en for the most up-to-date departure timetables. Tallinn is the country's main hub.

Popular connections

Domestic routes

Tallinn to other Estonian cities travel time:

Tallinn – Narva	2h 20m
Tallinn – Valga	3h 20m
Tallinn – Viljandi	2h 10m
Tallinn – Tartu	2h 05m
Tallinn – Paldiski	1h

International routes

International trains

There are no direct international trains from Tallinn to neighboring countries. However, there is a link with a transfer to Latvia via the Estonian border town of Valga.

Estonia to Latvia:

Tallinn - Valga - Riga line
The final station on the Tallinn-Valga line is within Estonian territory. Here you may change to a Latvian train that will take you straight to Riga or other Latvian locations.

Please check the timetables of both the Estonian Railways at elron.ee/en and the Latvian Railways at www.pv.lv/en since schedules are not always properly linked.

Ferry Routes

International Ferries

Tallinn has excellent links to Finland and Sweden. These ferries are not included in the Pass, although Eurail Pass holders may enjoy a discount on their journey. For additional information about these ferries and the discount, visit the perks portal:

Ferry to Finland: Tallinn - Helsinki

The ferry ride from Tallinn, Estonia, to Helsinki, Finland, takes between 2 and 3 hours. This route is provided by Tallink Silja, Viking Lines, and Eckerö Line.

Ferry to Sweden: Tallinn - Stockholm

The overnight ship from Tallinn, Estonia, to Stockholm, Sweden, takes roughly 16 hours. Viking Line and Tallink Silja provide this service.

Reservations

It is not possible to make a reservation using the Eurail reservation self-service system.

Locally in Estonia, at the rail station.

By sending an email

- When using a Eurail Pass, bookings for 2nd class are not feasible.
- Some lines have 1st class carriages that may be reserved by 1st class Pass holders. You may book a seat by sending an email to klienditugi@elron.ee 5 working days in advance. Enter the date, time, and route you wish to take.
- When the first session is sold out, it is possible to sit in the second class without making a reservation.
- When traveling with a 2nd class pass, it is possible to sit in 1st class if there are open seats in the 1st class cabin. This upgrade is only available on board and is subject to availability.

Good to know.

- A ticket inspector will examine your Pass on the train. You will be given a ticket, but it will be worth €0 and will be used only for Elron's administration.

Estonia Pass

- Spend your whole trip discovering Estonia by train.
- Standard pricing starts at $ 92

Global Pass

- You are free to visit Estonia and up to 32 other European countries
- Standard pricing begins at $ 211.

Hungary

Budapest is the main railway center of the Hungarian railway network, with three large stations. A 7,606 km network spreads from Budapest across the nation, with numerous links to significant cities.

Train Routes

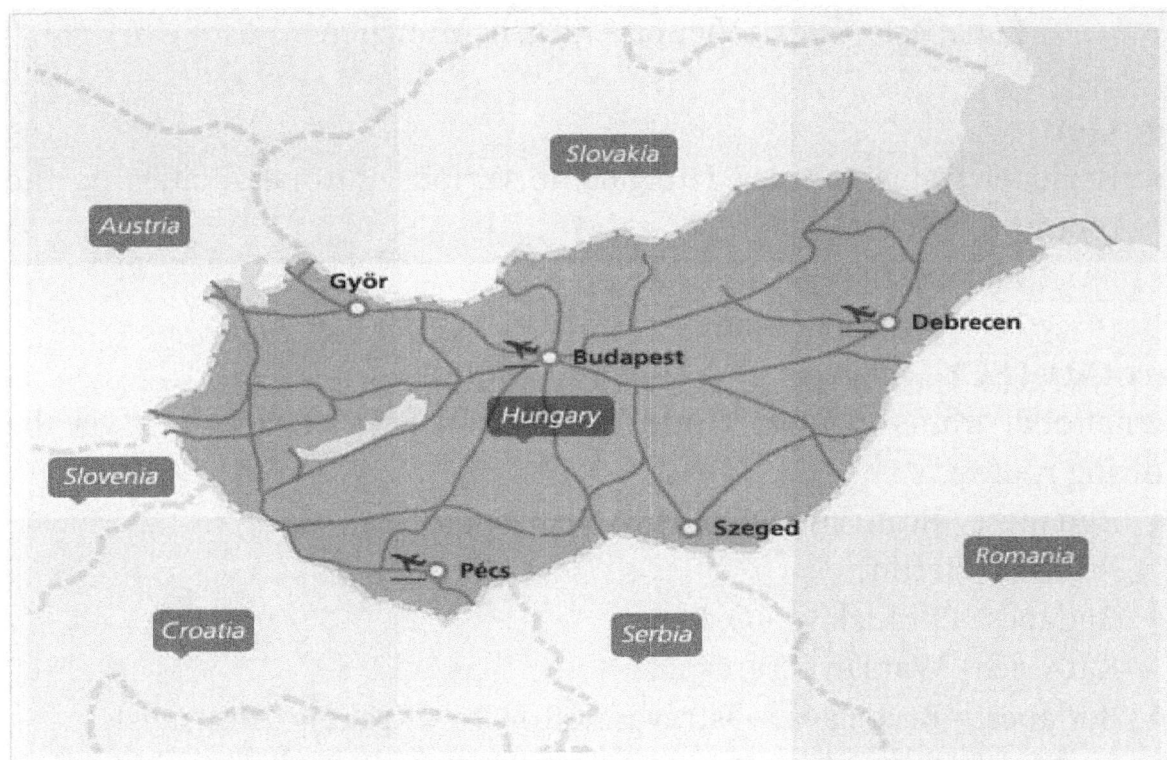

Train types in Hungary

If your Eurail Pass is valid in Hungary, you'll have access to MAV-START, the country's national railway firm. You'll also get access to the country's GYSEV/Raaberbahn trains.

Domestic Trains
Intercity trains in Hungary

- Regional (RE)
- Interregional (IR)
- EuroCity (EC)
- InterCity (IC)

International trains
- Railjet (RJ) international high-speed trains connect Hungary to various European cities via the following routes:
  - Budapest - Gyor - Vienna - Zürich/München

RegioJet
- RegioJet trains connect Hungary to various European cities on the route:
  - Budapest - Gyor - Viena - Brno - Prague

EuroCity (EC)
International trains connect Hungary to various European cities via the following routes:
- Budapest - Bratislava - Brno - Prague (- Berlin)
- Budapest - Bratislava - Ostrava - Katowice - Warsaw - Terespol
- Budapest - Bratislava - Ostrava - Katowice - Krakow - Przemysl
- Budapest - Gyor - Vienna
- Vienna - Gyor - Budapest -
- Oradea - Cluj Napoca
- Vienna - Gyor - Budapest - Debrecen - Satu Mare - Baia Mare

InterCity (IC)
- International trains connect Hungary to various European cities via the following routes:
  - Budapest - Kosice
  - Budapest - Graz

- Budapest - Ljubljana
- Budapest - Zagreb
- Budapest - Timisoara - Craiova - Bucharest
- Budapest - Arad - Sibiu - Brasov
- Budapest - Oradea - Cluj Napoca - Brasov
- Vienna - Gyor - Budapest - Debrecen - Zahony - Chop (Ukraine, only valid till Zahony)

Night Trains

EuroNight (EN)

- Night trains connect Hungary to various European cities via the following routes:
  - Budapest - Wroclaw - Berlin
  - Budapest - Prague
  - Budapest - Krakow - Warsaw
  - Budapest - Split (summer only)
  - Budapest - Oradea - Cluj Napoca
  - Budapest - Sibiu - Brasov - Bucharest
  - Vienna - Gyor - Budapest -
  - Brasov - Bucharest
  - Budapest - Craiova - Bucharest
  - Budapest - Salzburg - Munich - Stuttgart
  - Budapest - Zürich

Private railway companies

Private train lines run by the Austrian-Hungarian railway operator GYSEV (known in Austria as Raaberbahn) may also be accessed with your Interrail Pass.

GYSEV runs many rail lines, including;

- Sopron to Ebenfurth (Austria)
- Fertöszentmiklós to Neusiedl/See (Austria).

Popular connections

Domestic Routes

Intercity Regional Route (Reservations)

Route	Regional	Intercity (reservations)
Budapest to Debrecen	2h 50m	2h 15m
Budapest to Győr	1h 50m	1h 05m
Budapest to Pécs	4h (stopover)	2h 40m
Budapest to Szeged	3h	2h 10m

International routes

Route	Which train?	Travel time	Reservations
Budapest to Bratislava (Slovakia)	EuroCity	2h 35m	Optional
Budapest to Bucharest (Romania)	InterCity / EuroNight Ister	15h 40m / 15h 10m (overnight)	Required
Budapest to Ljubljana (Slovenia)	InterCity	7h 35m	Optional
Budapest to Munich (Germany)	RailJet	7h	Required
Budapest to Prague (Czech Republic)	EuroCity	6h 45m	Optional
Budapest to Vienna (Austria)	EuroCity / RailJet	2h 40m	Optional / Required

Budapest to Warsaw (Poland)	EuroCity / EuroNight	11h 20m / 13h 25m	Required
Budapest to Zagreb (Croatia)	InterCity	6h 35m	Optional

Reservations

Which trains in Hungary need reservations?
- No reservations: Regional trains (RE) and Interregio trains (IR)
- Domestic InterCity and EuroCity trains are optional.
- InterCity and EuroCity trains are required on some international routes.
- EuroNight is mandatory on all routes.

How can I book rail tickets in Hungary?
Reservation system
- Eurail

Eurail administration fees when booking via Eurail self-service:
- EUR 2,- per person per train
- Additional € 9,- per order
  (for paper tickets)

With railway carriers
- MAV (Hungarian railways): domestic trains
- BB (Austrian Railways): internal and international trains
- D (Czech railways): internal and international trains
- ZSSK (Slovakian Railways): internal and international trains

locally at the train station

Hungary Pass

- Use your whole trip to explore Hungary by train.
- Standard pricing starts at $ 92.

Global Pass

- You are free to tour Hungary and up to 32 other European countries.
- Standard pricing begins at $ 211.

Hungary Tips and Techniques

Quick Facts

- Budapest is the capital city.
- Population: ten million
- language: Hungarian.
- Currency: Hungarian Forint (HUF)
- Dialing code: +36

MAV-START Business Lounge

First-class Eurail ticket members get free access to the VIP lounge at Budapest Keleti Railway Station.

Airport-to-station connections

If you arrive in Hungary by plane, you may easily reach Budapest city center by rail from Ferihegy International Airport Terminal 1.

Hungary has a Eurail help office

You may get assistance with your Eurail pass at the aid office in Budapest, József Attila str. 16.

Budapest's major rail stations

Budapest is a rail travel hub, with four major stations:

- Keleti is in the east. The primary international and intercity train station in Budapest.
- Nyugati is located in the north.
- Deli: Located in the west.
- Kelenföld is located in the southwest.

Latvia

It's time to discover northern Europe with a Eurail Pass! The Latvian railway carrier takes you all throughout the nation, from the Baltic Sea to ancient cities and magnificent nature.

Routes Map

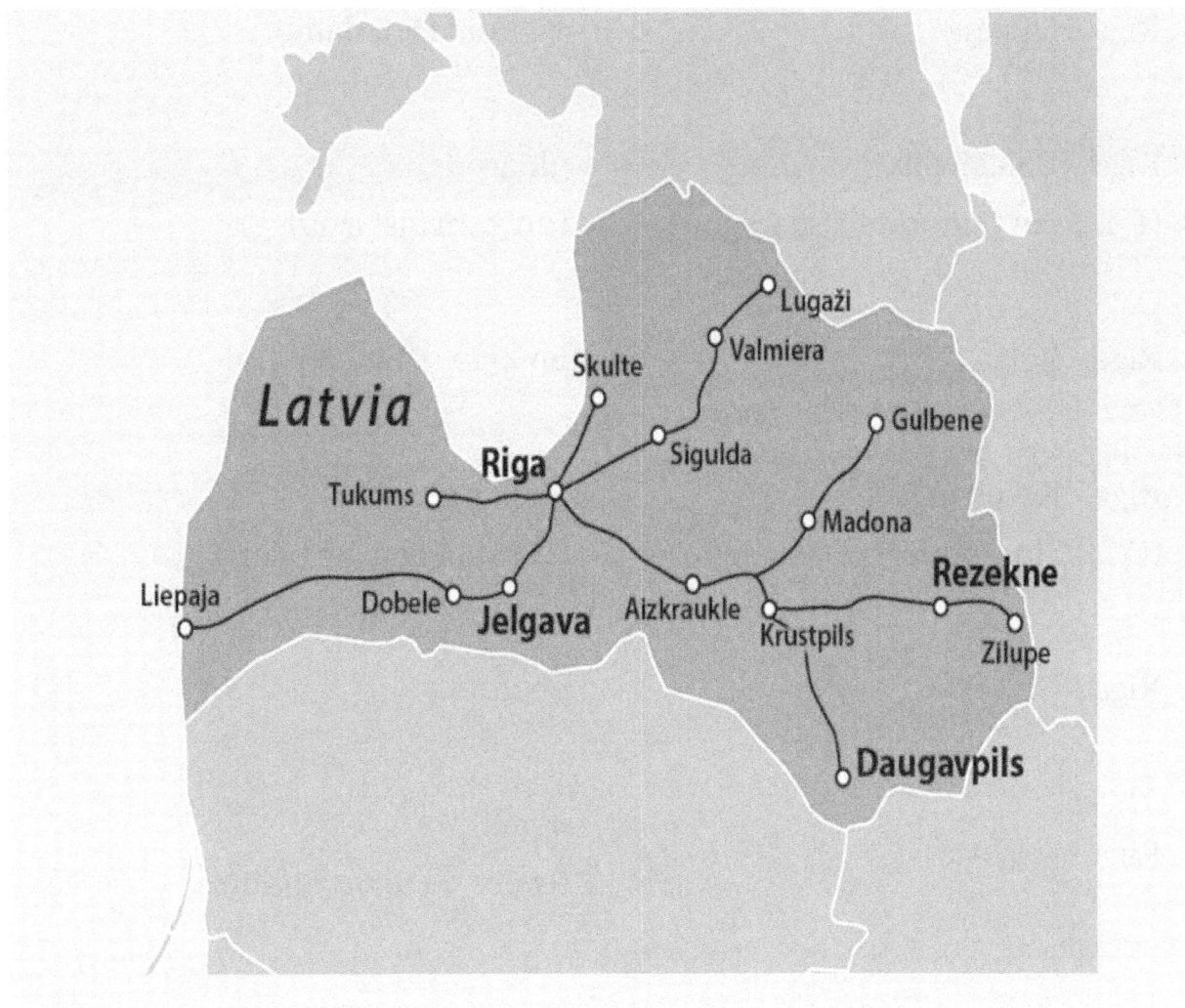

Train Types in Latvia

Domestic Trains

Pasaieru Vilciens operates trains in Latvia (www.pv.lv/en). Riga is the main hub. All trains in Latvia are regional, and most cannot be reserved.

Riga to other Latvian cities average travel time:

Riga - Liepaja	3h 20m (not daily)
Riga - Daugavpils (€ 1.40 in Comfort class wagon)	3h 20m (2h 45m fast service)
Riga - Valga	2h 45m
Riga - Rezekne (€ 1.40 in Comfort class wagon)	3h 35m (2h 45m fast service)
Riga - Gulbene	3h 20m
Riga - Jelgava	45m (every 30 to 60 minutes)
Riga - Jurmala (beach) *Main stations: Majori and Dubulti*	30m (every 30 minutes)

International Trains

International trains

There are no direct international trains from Latvia to neighboring nations. There are, nevertheless, links (with a change of trains) to Estonia and Lithuania.

Latvia to Estonia: Riga - Valga line

The last station on the Riga-Valga line is within Estonian territory. From here, you may change to an Estonian train that will take you straight to Tallinn or other places in Estonia.

Please check the timetables of both the Latvian Railways at www.pv.lv/en and the Estonian Railways at elron.ee/en since schedules are not always properly linked.

Latvia to Lithuania: Riga - Daugavpils line

There is currently no international rail service connecting these two nations. You may take a bus to Turmantas in Latvia and then change to a Lithuanian train that will take you to Vilnius or other places in Lithuania (please note that these busses are not included in your Pass).

Ferry

International ferries

Latvia has excellent links to Sweden and Germany. These ferries are not included in the Pass, although Pass holder can get a discount on their journey. For additional information about these ferries,

Ferries to Germany:
- Liepaja (Latvia) - Travemunde,
  (Germany): the route offered by Stena Line takes 27 hours

Ferries to Sweden
- Riga (Latvia) - Stockholm (Sweden): Tallink Silja operates this route, which takes around 17 hours.

- Stena Line operates the route Ventspils (Latvia) - Nynäshamm (Sweden), which takes around 7,5 hours.

Reservations

Reservations in Latvia
Reservations are permitted on two routes in Latvia; reservations are not possible on any other trains:

Riga - Daugavpils - Indra
- There is a train on this route once a day with a comfort class portion (additional price € 1.40). Reservations are strongly advised for this train.

- This train also stops at the following stations: Ogre, Aizkraukle, Plavinas, Krustpils, and Lvani.

Riga - Rezekne II
- There is a train on this route once a day with a comfort class portion (additional price € 1.40). Reservations are strongly advised for this train.

- This is only applicable for a portion of the route:
  - Riga - Rezekne.
- This train also stops at the following stations: Ogre, Aizkraukle, Pavias, Krustpils, and Vijāni.

How to Make Reservations:
Phone: +371 90000 1222
Please keep in mind that you can make reservations up to one hour before the train's departure.

Latvian Pass

- Latvia Pass allows you to travel by train across Latvia.
- Discounts are provided for students, seniors, and families.
- Prices start at $ 59.

Global Pass

- Have the flexibility to visit Latvia and up to 32 additional European countries.
- There are discounts for
  - children, seniors, and families.
- Prices begin at $ 211.

Latvian Tips & Tricks

Latvian rail stations
- The central railway station in Riga is Latvia's principal station. All domestic lines depart from this station. You may utilize the following services:

Luggage Lockers
- Riga Central Station has luggage storage.

Lost and Found
- The "Pasazieru vilciens" Customer Service Centre at Riga Central Station handles lost and found items. In the event of a lost or discovered item, please call +371 67232135.

Service Center
- Riga Railway Station Service Centre, Stacijas laukums 2.
- Phone: +371 67232135
- Daily hours are 7:00-19:00.

Pass Benefits in Latvia
Benefits of an Interrail Pass include:
- Discounted ferry passage to Germany and Sweden

Luxembourg

Luxembourg is centrally located in Europe and has an outstanding rail network. With your Interrail pass, you can get to know a small yet modern, cosmopolitan, and multicultural nation. Explore the capital's various eateries and bars. Stroll through the historic center's narrow streets, explore walking trails in the north, industrial culture in the south, or the beautiful Moselle Valley. Furthermore, beginning of March 2020, bus, train, and tram travel will be free nationwide.

Train types in Luxembourg

CFL (Société Nationale des Chemins de Fer Luxembourgeois), the Grand Duchy's national railway company, operates regional trains and buses across the Grand Duchy. International trains link Luxembourg to cities in neighboring nations. The Eurail timetable contains train timings for Luxembourg.

A valid Luxembourg Pass can be used on any CFL train service. One Country Pass and Global Pass holders do not need to utilize the Pass to travel by rail in 2nd Class since all second class public transportation in Luxembourg, including funiculars, trams, and trains, is free. Pass holders in first class need to use the Pass if they travel in first class in Luxembourg. Domestic Trains in Luxembourg

RegionalBahn (RB)
- Regular services stop at every station along the route.
- There is no need for a reservation.

Regional Express (RE)
- Similar to RegionalBahn trains, but with fewer stops at stations along the route.
- There is no need for a reservation.

CFL buses (BUS)
- In Luxembourg, a fleet of 60 buses complements the rail network.
- There is no need for a reservation.

City buses, regional buses, trams, and funiculars
- These modes of public transportation are completely free.
- International trains in Luxembourg

InterCity (IC)
Trains link Luxembourg to Liège and Brussels in Belgium.
- The RB and RE trains link Luxembourg to Koblenz and Düsseldorf in Germany, as well as Metz and Nancy in France.
- Reservations are optional. If you're going to be traveling at a busy time, I suggest preparing one.

TGV (TGV)
For travel between Luxembourg and Paris (France).
- Reservations are required for this train, which might become completely booked. Because there are only a limited number of seats available for Pass members, I suggest making your reservation three months in advance to prevent disappointment.

CFL International Buses (BUS)
- Two international bus services supplement Luxembourg's rail network.
- Easy access from Luxembourg Central Station to saarbrücken and Gare Lorraine TGV.

A reservation is needed.

Popular connections

International routes

Travel to and from Luxembourg is possible from the following prominent European cities:

Route	Which train?	Travel time	Reservations
Luxembourg City to Brussels (Belgium)	InterCity	3 hours	Optional
Luxembourg City to Koblenz (Germany)	InterCity	2 hours	Optional
Luxembourg City to Paris (France)	TGV	2 hours	Required

Reservations

How can I book rail tickets in Luxembourg?
- Online: via the Reservation Service.
- At large rail stations, use a ticket office or a self-service machine.
- by phone: call the CFL call center, which is open Monday through Friday from 7:00 a.m. to 19:00 p.m. Closed on public holidays.

What can I anticipate if I contact CFL?

1. Dial +352 2489 2489 to reach CFL.

2. You'll hear a menu in German, English and French.

3. Select "2" for reservations and train information.

4. You may have your bookings sent to any European country for $ 7. You can pick them up at Luxembourg's main rail station for a $5 booking charge.

Luxembourg Pass

- With only one pass, you can visit Belgium, the Netherlands, and Luxembourg.
- Standard pricing starts at € 120.

Global Pass

- Feel free to go to the Benelux and up to 30 additional European nations.
- Standard pricing begins at $ 211.

Luxembourg Tricks & Tips

Quick Facts

- Capital: Luxembourg City
- Languages: French, German, Luxembourgish
- Currency: Euro (EUR)
- +352: dialing code.

Luxembourg's hub stations

Luxembourg is the major hub station in Luxembourg. From here, you can connect to trains and buses that will transport you around Luxembourg and to many foreign locations.

Station Facilities

Luxembourg has great amenities, including:

- Luggage lockers
- Foreign exchange desks
- Restaurants and cafés
- ATM cash machines in tourist information offices
- Elevators and escalators
- Shops
- Access for travelers with disabilities.

Lithuania

Want to embark on an excursion to the greatest parts of Lithuania? Most places in Lithuania can be reached by train! From vibrant Vilnius to the natural beauties of Klaipeda and beyond, the Lithuanian train network links you to neighboring Poland and a load of local highlights.

Routes Map

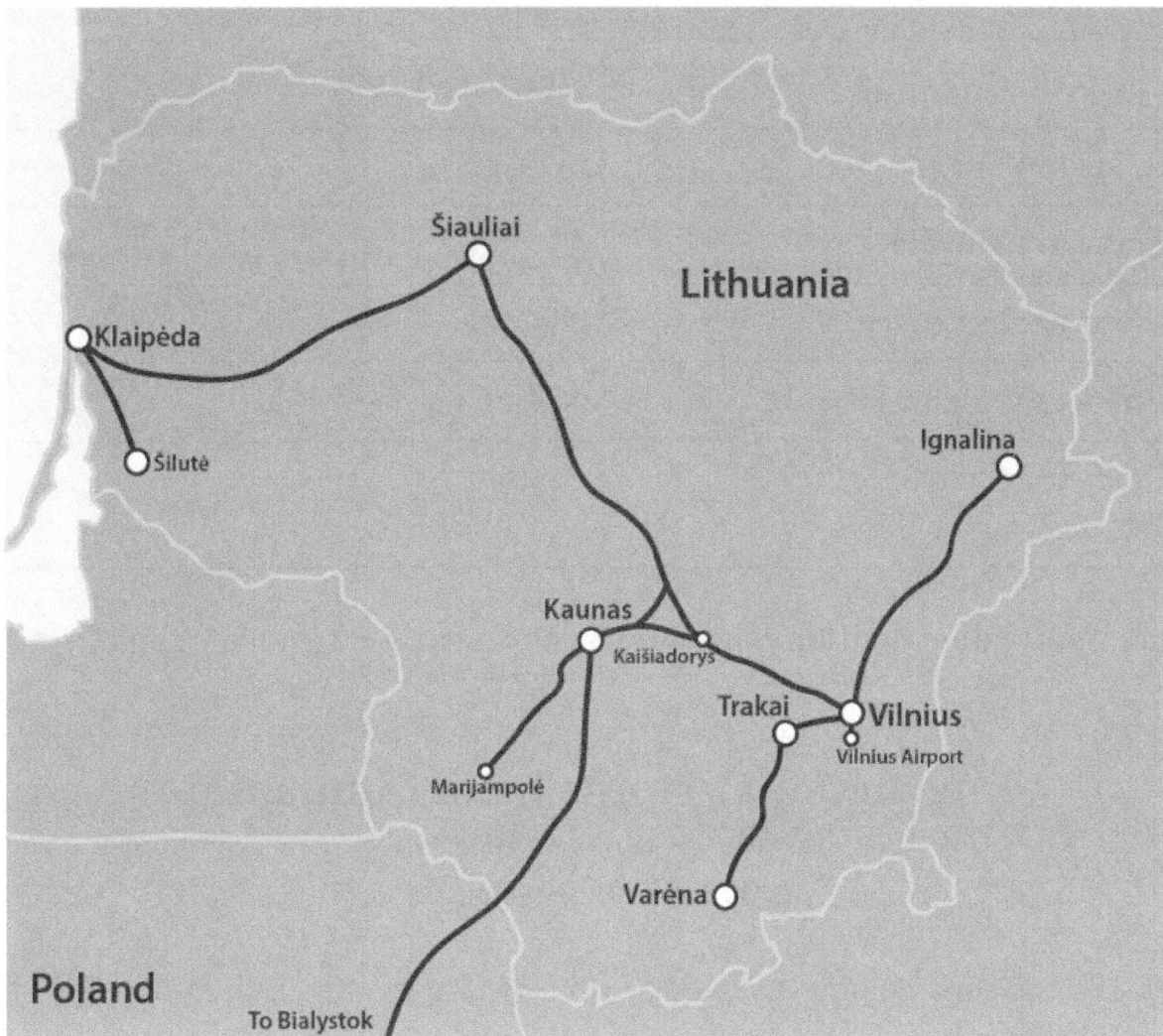

Train types in Lithuania

- Domestic trains in Lithuania are mostly operated by LGT Link.
- Vilnius Railway Station is the country's biggest station and the main train traffic center.
- There is an 8-times-daily direct rail connection from Vilnius airport to this central station that takes 7 minutes and costs EUR 0.80.
- Other major stations are located in Klaipeda, Radvilikis, and Kaunas.
- Eurail Passes are not usable on buses or trams.

Travel times in Lithuania:

Route	Travel Time
Vilnius to Kaunas	1h 20m
Vilnius to Klaipeda	4h 25m
Vilnius to Slauliai	2h 30m
Vilnius to Visaginas	2h 15m
Vilnius to Mockava (train to Kraków)	2h 30m

More information on train routes in Lithuania can be found at ltglink.lt/en.

International Trains from Lithuania:

Vilnius - Kaunas - Mockava -
Warsaw - Krakow (Poland).

- Passengers change trains at Mockava, near the Lithuanian-Polish border.
- A Lithuanian train travels the route Vilnius-Kaunas-Mockava.

- A Polish train travels the route Mockava-Warsaw-Krakow.
- These trains operate every day.
- Reservations are necessary.
  - Reservations may only be made at the train station for the segment between Vilnius and Mockava.
  - Reservations for the segment between the Polish border station Trakiszki and Krakow can be purchased online in the Eurail reservation system and via PKP Intercity at intercity.pl.
- Bikes and luggage can be transported on board if space allows. There is a 35kg luggage restriction, however, you may buy an extra luggage allowance.

Reservations

In Lithuania, reservations are not required for rail travel. Reservations are strongly advised for the Vilnius-Klaipeda route due to high demand.

Route	What is included:
Vilnius - Klaipeda	Drinks and snacks are available in the first class. For sale with a second-class ticket.
Vilnius - Klaipėda - Nida (Pajrio ekspresas) Summer service only	Drinks and snacks are available in the first class. For sale with a second-class ticket. Bus transfer from Klaipeda to Nida

Vilnius - Klaipėda - Palanga (Pajrio ekspresas) Summer service only	Drinks and snacks are available in the first class. For sale with a second-class ticket. Bus transfer from Klaipeda to Palanga

How to book a Reservations
At the train station in Lithuania.

Lithuania Pass

Get your Lithuania Pass
- Spend your whole trip visiting Lithuania by train.
- Standard pricing begins at $ 59.

Global Pass
- Feel free to tour Lithuania, as well as the other 32 European countries.
- Standard pricing begins at $ 211.

Montenegro

Montenegro is worth a visit due to its architectural and cultural heritage, variety of landscapes and temperatures, and unspoiled environment. There are sandy beaches and a dynamic nightlife along the Adriatic coast. The primary railway destinations are the capital Podgorica and the beach city Bar.

Routes Map

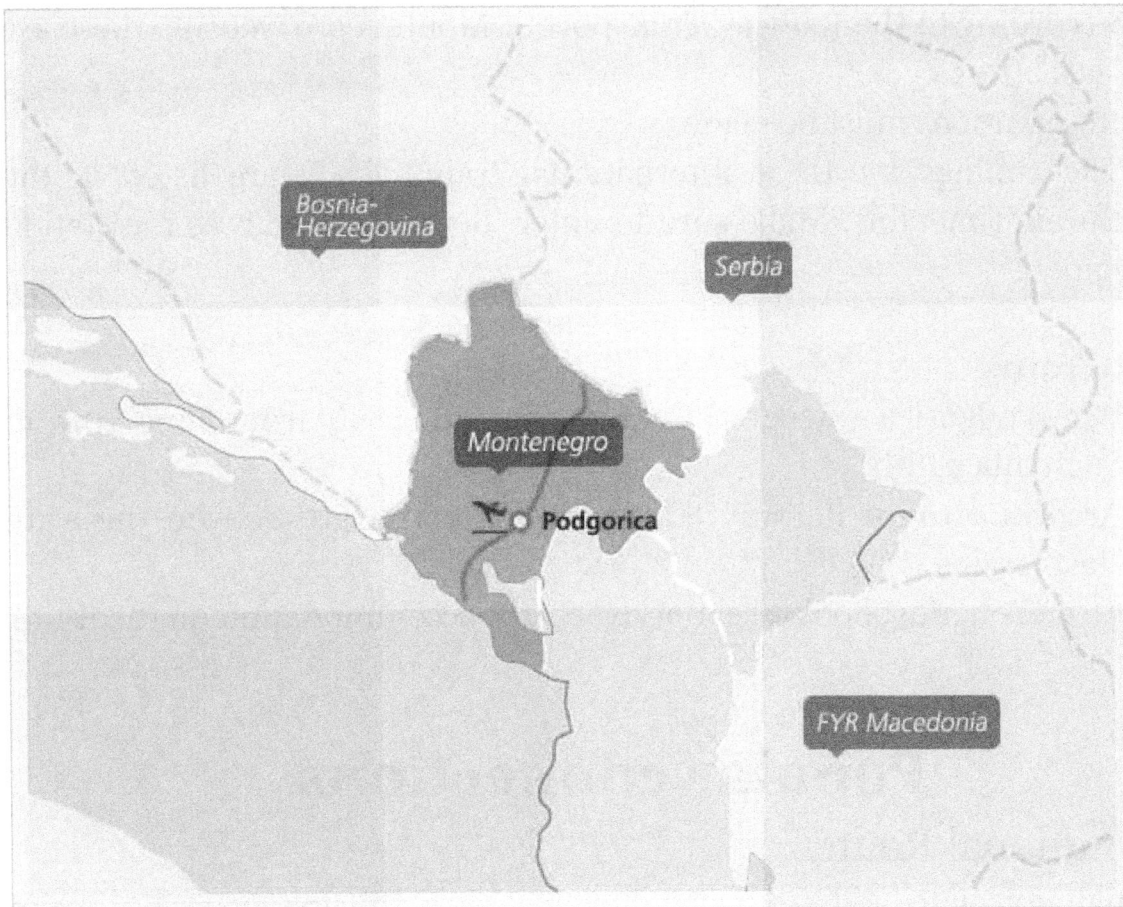

Train types in Montenegro

Domestic Train

Regional trains

- Trains travel between Bar, Podgorica, Bijelo Polje, and Niki.
- Trains are listed as "local" on the Railway Transport of Montenegro website.
- There is no need for a reservation.

International trains

- Bar- Podgorica - Beograd Centar - Zemun (Daily)
- According to the Railway Transport of Montenegro website, these are "fast" trains.
- Reservations must be made.
- The timings for these international trains (INT) are listed in the Eurail Timetable. Make sure to enter 'Beograd Centar' as the station name.

Night Trains

- Bar- Podgorica - Beograd Centar - Zemun (Daily from June 20th to September 18th)
- According to the Railway Transport of Montenegro website, these are "fast" trains.
   - You must book a seat or overnight accommodation on the train.

Popular connections

International Routes

You may travel to and from Montenegro from the following European cities:

Routes	Which Train?	Travel time	Reservations

Bar to Belgrade (Serbia)	International Train / Night Train	11h / 11h (overnight)	Mandatory
Podgorica to Belgrade (Serbia)	International Train / Night Train	10h / 10h (overnight)	Mandatory

Reservations

How can I book rail tickets in Montenegro?

It is not possible to make a reservation using the Eurail reservation self-service system.

Locally, at the Montenegrin rail station.

Good to know.
The only trains in Montenegro that need reservations are the day and night trains to Belgrade and Zemun (Serbia). Plan ahead of time to ensure that you can make your plans on a timetable.

Montenegro Pass

Global Pass
- You are free to visit Montenegro and up to 32 other European countries.
- Standard pricing begins at $ 211.

Montenegrin Tricks and Tips

Quick Facts

- Capital: Podgorica
- Population: 625,000
- Language: Montenegrin
- Currency: Euro (EUR)
- +382: dialing code.

Norway

Norway's dazzling fjords and mountains provide the most breathtaking vistas in Europe, and you can see them all on scenic rail lines. Make your journey complete by visiting these intriguing towns and cities. Norway is an excellent choice for an exciting European vacation.

Routes Map

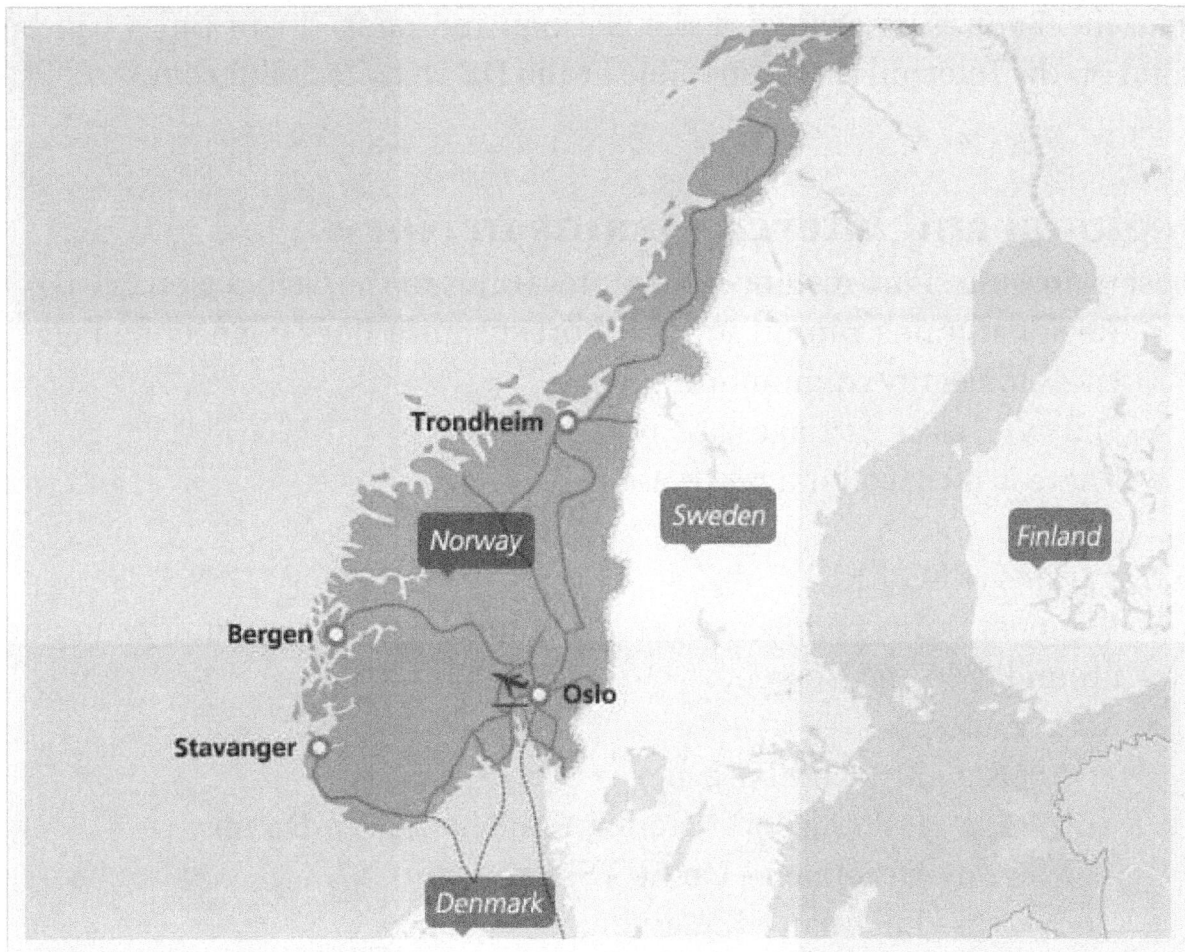

Train Types in Norway

Trains operated by VY Railways, GoAhead Norge, and SJ are expected to impress. They're quite fantastic. They're modern, comfy, and ready to transport you across the nation at any time of day. The Eurail Timetable may be used to check train timetables in Norway.

Reservations for most Norwegian trains are marked as optional in the Timetable. However, I recommend that you always make reservations in Norway since trains are often overcrowded.

Deutsche Bahn is in charge of the German railroads. Train times can be found on the Interrail train timetable or the DB website, bahn.com.

Regional and intercity trains in Norway

Local trains and short-distance commuter trains in the Oslo region (SUB)

- Regional trains run on several short-distance lines connecting bigger cities to nearby communities.
- Only 2nd class carriages are available.
- There is no need for a reservation.

VY Tåg trains (REG / RE)

- Regional trains connect larger cities and smaller communities in and around Oslo and Bergen.
- Main routes:
    - Oslo - Myrdal - Bergen
    - Oslo - Oslo Airport - Hamar - Lillehammer - Dombs
    - Oslo - Drammen - Larvik - Skien
    - Oslo - Lillestrm - Kongsvinger
    - Oslo - Moss - Fredrikstad - Halden
- Some routes need reservations.

Go-Ahead Norge trains (REG/ RE)

- Regional trains connect larger cities and smaller communities between Oslo and Stavanger.
- Operating on three routes:
  - Oslo - Kristiansand - Stavanger
  - Stavanger - Egersund
  - Nelaug - Arendal
- Some routes need reservations.

SJ Norge trains (REG)

- Regional trains run on Dovrebanen, Rosbanen, Raumabanen, and Nordlandsbanen, while local trains run on Trnderbanen and Merkerbanen.
- The main routes are:
  - Oslo - Dombås - Trondheim.
  - Hamar - Rros - Trondheim
  - Trondheim - Mo I Rana - Bodø
  - Trondheim - Hell - Storlien (Sweden)
- Some routes need reservations.

Gjovikbanen AS (REG)

- Regional rail from Oslo to Gjvik, via Nordmarka.
- Reservations are optional.

Only the reservation fee is required with a Eurail Pass valid in Norway.

Bus services in Norway
Veøy buss

- There is a bus service from andalsnes to Molde.
- On the bus, tickets are always available for purchase.
- Eurail Pass holders get a 50% discount.

International trains

SJ high-speed
- Trains from Oslo to Stockholm (Sweden)
- Reservations must be made.

VY Regiontog day trains (REG)
- Trains from Oslo to Gothenburg (Sweden) (REG)
- Reservations are optional.

SJ Norge trains (REG)
- Trains from Trondheim to Storlien (Sweden)
- Reservations are not required.

Night Trains in Norway

Domestic night trains (REG)
- Domestic overnight trains run on the following routes:
  - Oslo - Stavanger (GoAhead Nordic).
  - Oslo - Bergen (VY Tog)
  - Oslo - Trondheim (SJ Norge)
  - Trondheim - Bodø (SJ Norge)
- Sleep in a comfortable cabin and wake up to breathtaking sights passing by your train window.
- The keys to the sleeping compartments are obtained at the onboard café (Meny Kafé).
- You must book a bed or a seat in advance.

Go-Ahead Norge night train (REG).
- Domestic overnight train between Oslo and Stavanger
- Comfortable beds, maximum of two adults and two children per compartment
- Free water and earplugs
- You must book a bed in advance.

Tourist Trains in Norway

Flåm Railway (RE)

- A very wild and picturesque rail route.
- Connects the alpine railway station Myrdal to Flåm, lying 865 meters lower in the picturesque Aurlandsfjord.
- Rail passes do not cover this, although holders of a Eurail Pass get a 30% discount.
- Pre-purchase your ticket by phoning the Entur customer service line at +47 61 27 90 88.

Popular connections

Domestic routes

Here are the regional train lines in Norway that connect major cities and are covered by the Eurail Pass.

Route	Time
Oslo to Bergen	7h
Oslo to Stavanger	7h 45m
Oslo to Trondheim	6h 40m
Trondheim to Bodø	10h

International Routes

Travel to and from Norway is possible from the following popular European cities:

Route	Train/ferry	Duration	Reservations
Bergen,	Fjordline ferry	2h to 17h	required

Kristiansand, or Stavanger to Hirtshals (Denmark)			
Oslo to Gothenburg (Sweden)	VY Regiontog	3h 30m	Optional
Oslo to Stockholm (Sweden)	SJ High Speed	5h 30m	Required
Trondheim to Storlien	SJ Norge	1h 40m	Not Required
Narvik to Stockholm	VY Night train	18h 15m	required

To get from Denmark to Norway by rail, take a regional train from Copenhagen (Denmark) to Gothenburg (Sweden). Then take the direct VY Regiontog indicated in the preceding table. This will take less than 9 hours overall. Reservations are needed for trains between Sweden and Norway.

Reservations

I highly advise you to book a seat on the long-distance trains since they might fill up rapidly, particularly during peak season.

Ways to make reservations for trains in Norway

Reservation system for Eurail

- Eurail
    - Regiontog

Booking via Eurail self-service costs administrative fees.
- EUR 2,- per person per train
- Additional € 9,- per order
  (for paper tickets)

With railway carriers
- Entur Domestic trains

Locally in Norway, at the rail station
- By phoning the Entur call center at +47 61 27 90 88
  (press 9 for English services).

Opening hours:
Monday through Friday, 07:00 a.m. - 11:00 p.m.
Saturday: 08:00 - 21:00
Sunday: 08:00 - 23:00
Bank holiday hours are reduced.

Enter Call Center handles reservations for all Norwegian rail operators (excluding Flytoget AS). You may buy tickets or seat reservations for the following train companies: Vy (Vygruppen AS), GAN (Go Ahead Nordic AS), and SJ (SJ Norge AS).

Seat reservations are normally available up to 90 days in advance and are not required in Norway. Seat reservations are strongly advised when available. During the summer, popular trains to and from popular places (for example, the Oslo-Bergen Line) are often overcrowded.

Payment
They only take credit cards (Visa, MasterCard, and American Express). You must pay immediately, When you make a reservation.

Ticket collecting
- Using a home print solution is the most convenient method to get your trip documentation and receipts. You will get an e-mail with

information and an attached PDF with your travel papers. You may either present the digital papers on your smartphone or tablet or print your tickets at home and bring them aboard to show the train management (note: if you pick the home print option, your tickets will not be accessible for print at TVM's).

- Instead of printing tickets at home, you may have them printed at self-service ticket vending machines (TVMs). You will get an email containing travel information, a receipt for your purchase, and a booking reference/Order ID that can be used at the TVMs for pick up.
- Many rail stations in Norway have TVMs. For additional information and station specifics, please visit Bane NOR at banenor.no for a list of stations in Norway. Norway's manned rail stations are Oslo S, Oslo Airport Gardermoen, Bergen, Trondheim, and Stavanger.

Good to know
- first-class Pass holders pay no reservation cost on domestic day trips. However, first-class pass holders must have a seat reservation in upgraded compartments (Komfort, Pluss, or Premium - depending on the train provider). This is free to book, but you must book locally.
- There is no difference between first and second class on night trains.
- The Komfort Night location is only available on the Srlandsbanen (Oslo-Kristiansand-Stavanger-Oslo) night train. It is offered all nights except Saturday night to Sunday morning and costs 230 NOK (about €25) and may only be booked in Norway.

Norway Pass

- Spend your whole trip visiting Norway by train.
- Standard pricing begins at $ 169.

Global Pass

- Have the flexibility to travel to Norway and up to 32 additional European countries.

- Standard pricing begins at $ 211.

Scandinavia Pass

- With one Eurail pass, you may travel to Norway, Denmark, Sweden, and Finland.
- Standard pricing starts at $ 190.

Norway Tips and Techniques

The major rail stations in Norway

The capital city of Norway is the train traffic center. Oslo Central Station, or "Oslo S" for short, links Norway's main cities as well as overseas destinations.

Norway's railway stations provide excellent facilities:

- ATMs and foreign exchange desks
- Cafés, restaurants, and shops
- tourist information
- Elevators and escalators
- Good accessibility for disabled travelers

Norwegian railway companies

Your Interrail Pass includes three railway companies in Norway: VY, Go Ahead Norge, and SJ.

You can reserve all trains from these three carriers via Entur, either by phone or at their ticket counters at the train station. Reservations are required for VY Tog regional trains between Oslo and Bergen. Reservations are not required for other long-distance and regional trains, but they are strongly advised because trains can fill up quickly!

Romania

Travel by rail across Romania to learn about its history and beauty. Expect to visit various landscapes with gorgeous scenery, intriguing towns, and stunning castles. A trip to Romania will leave you with memories that you will never forget.

Route Map

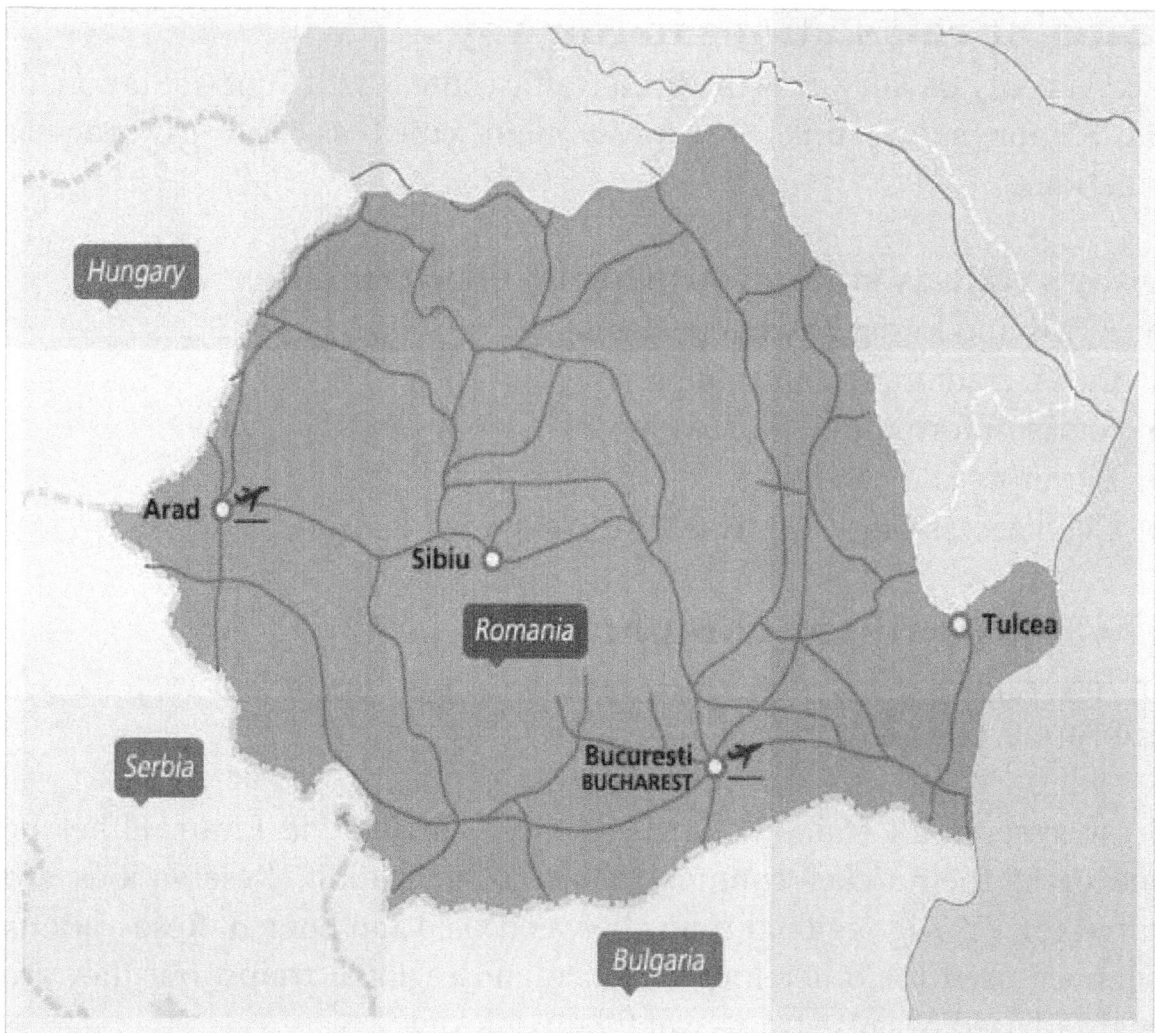

Train types in Romania

You can travel freely across Romania on trains operated by the Romanian railway firm CFR (Căile Ferate Române) at www.cfrcalatori.ro/en In addition to these local services, there are international trains to neighboring countries. Timetables for Romanian trains can be found in the Eurail timetable or on the CFR website.

Domestic Trains

Regional and intercity trains in Romania

Regio (RE)

- Slow trains with numerous stops link smaller towns and villages along commuter routes.
- Bicycles are allowed on board. You must purchase a bicycle ticket.
- Formerly known as "Personal" trains.
- There is no need for a reservation.

InterRegio (IR)

- Trains that go faster and stop at significant towns and cities.
- Bicycles are allowed on board. You must purchase a bicycle ticket.
- Previously known as "Rapid" and "Accelerate" trains.
- On several routes, reservations are necessary.

Intercity (IC)

- Trains link Romania's major cities.
- They also connect to overseas locations, namely Budapest.
- Reservations are necessary.

Special (S)

- Vintage tourist trains on picturesque routes.
- Exceptional conditions apply.

International Trains in Romania

InterCity (IC)

- Bucharest - Craiova - Timisoara - Arad - Budapest
- Timisoara - Arad - Budapest
- Brasov - Cluj Napoca - Oradea - Budapest

EuroCity (EC)

- Cluj-Napoca - Oradea - Budapest - Vienna
- Baia Mare - Satu Mare - Debrecen - Budapest - Vienna

Other international trains

- Bucharest - Ruse - Sofia (from June 21st to October 9th)
- Bucharest - Ruse - Varna (from June 21st to October 9th)
- Bucharest - Ruse (all year)
- Craiova - Vidin (Bulgaria)

Domestic Night Trains in Romania

Romania boasts one of Europe's most comprehensive night rail networks, with trains traveling to every part of the country. There are several international night rail services as well.

Intercity (IC) and InterRegio (IR) night trains

- Couchettes and sleepers have been installed on Intercity and InterRegio trains on nighttime runs.
- Reservations are necessary.
- You may use the following domestic night train routes:
    - Bucharest - Craiova - Timisoara
    - Bucharest - Brasov - -Beclean pe somes - Sighetu Marmatiei
    - Bucharest - Brasov - - Beclean pe somes - Baia Mare
    - Bucharest - Brasov - Cluj Napoca -

Oradea - Satu Mare
- ○ Bucharest - Ploiesti - Buzau -
  - Suceava - Vatra Dornei
- ○ Bucharest - Buzau - Buzau - Iasi
- ○ Timisoara - Arad - Cluj Napoca -
  Suceava - Iasi

- Domestic night trains operate exclusively during the summer season:
  - ○ Mangalia - Constanta -
    Beclean pe somes - Baia Mare -
    Satu Mare
  - ○ Constanta - Bucharest - Brasov -
    Cluj Napoca - Oradea
  - ○ Mangalia - Constanta - Bucharest -
    Craiova - Timisoara - Arad
  - ○ Constanta - Pascani - Suceava

International Night Trains in Romania
EuroNight (EN)
- International night train linking Bucharest with Budapest (Hungary) and Vienna (Austria).
- Reservations are necessary.
- You may use the following domestic night train routes:
  - ○ Bucharest - Brasov - Sibiu - Budapest
  - ○ Bucharest - Craiova -
    - Timisoara - Budapest (- Vienna)
  - ○ Bucharest - Brasov - Sighisoara -
    Budapest - Vienna
  - ○ Cluj-Napoca - Oradea - Budapest - Vienna
  - ○ Brasov - Miercurea Ciuc -
    Oradea - Budapest

- Other night trains
  - ○ Bucharest - Istanbul Halkali (Summer only)

Popular connections

Domestic Routes

Route	Duration (Regional Train)	Reservations (Intercity)
Bucharest to Brasov	2 h 30 m	Required
Bucharest to Timisoara	20 h	Required
Bucharest to Cluj-Napoca	8h 30m	Required
Bucharest to Constanta	2 h	Required
Bucharest to Iasi	6 h	Required
Bucharest to Sibiu	5h 40m	Required

International routes

Here are several direct rail lines connecting Romania with prominent cities in other European countries:

Route	Which train?	Duration	Reservations
Brasov to Budapest (Hungary)	Intercity / EuroNight	13h (overnight)	Required
Bucharest to Budapest (Hungary) is required	Intercity / EuroNight	16h / 15h 30m (overnight)	Required

Bucharest to Sofia (Bulgaria)*	International Train	9h 30m	Required
Bucharest to Vienna (Austria)	EuroNight	18h 30m (overnight)	Required
Bucharest to Istanbul (Turkey)	Night Train	19h 45m (overnight)	Required
Cluj to Budapest (Hungary)	EuroCity / Night Train	7h30m / 8h30m (overnight)	Required

*The train from Bucharest to Istanbul exits at Istanbul Halkali station, from whence you can take a metro/Marmaray train to the city center and beneath the Bosphorus to the Asian side. Make sure you have Turkish Lira notes on hand since most metro ticket machines do not accept bank cards.

Reservations

How can I book rail tickets in Romania?
Reservation system for Eurail
- Eurail
- Interregio, Euro Night, and domestic night trains

Booking via Eurail self-service administrative fees costs.
- EUR 2,- per person per train
- Additional € 9,- per order
- (for paper tickets)

With railway carriers
ÖBB (Austrian Railways):
- Some international trains to Hungary and Austria.

Locally in Romania, at the rail station

By phone
- Through the Deutsche Bahn booking center. You can reach DB at +49 1806 996 633 24 /7

Romania Pass

- Use your whole holiday to explore Romania by train.
- Standard pricing starts at $ 92.

Global Pass

- Feel free to travel throughout Romania and up to 32 other European countries.
- Standard pricing begins at $ 211.

Romanian Tips & Tricks

Hotel Discounts

With a valid Eurail pass in Romania, you may get a 10% discount at the following hotels:
- Hotel Alexandros in Busteni

Quick facts
- Capital: Bucharest (local spelling: Bucureşti)
- Population: 20.1 million
- Language: Romanian
- Currency: Romanian Leu (RON)
- dialing code: +40

Slovakia

Train travel is an excellent way to see Slovakia's untainted landscapes and rich folk culture. The welcoming youthful city of Bratislava is readily accessible with your Eurail Pass. Enjoy the medieval town of Kosice in east Slovakia and marvel at the mineral-rich Tiavnica mountain ranges. While you're here, try some Slovak wines from the Carpathian areas.

Routes Map

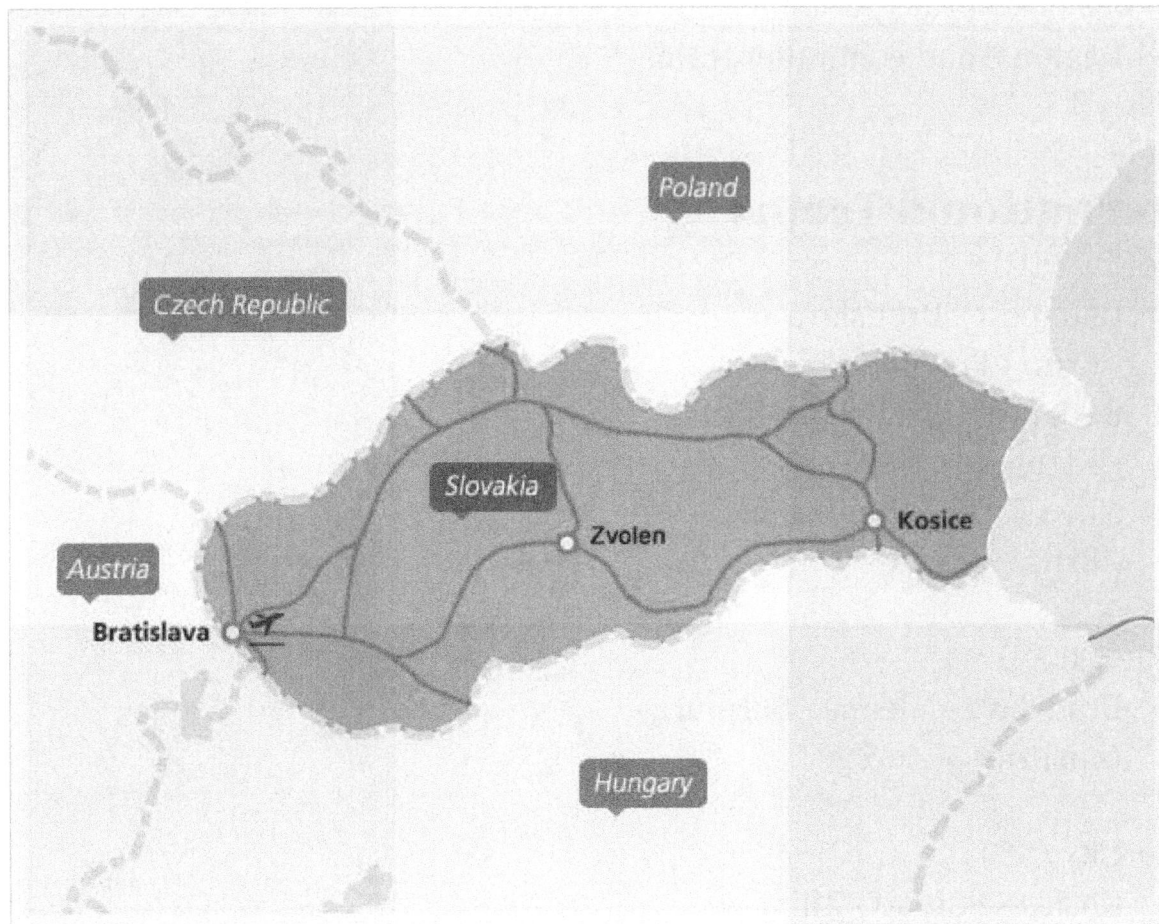

Train types

Domestic Trains

Eurocity (EC) and InterCity (IC)
- Intercity trains run between major cities.
- Reservations are necessary.

Express (Ex), Rychlik (R), and
Regionálny Rychlik (RR)
- Long-distance interregional trains
- Reservations are only necessary in first class.

Regional fast rail (REX) and Osobn Vlak (Os)
- Regional and commuter trains

International Trains

EuroCity (EC)
- Budapest - Bratislava -
  - Brno - Prague - (Berlin)
- Budapest - Bratislava - Ostrava -
  - Katowice - Krakow - Przemysl
- Nove Zamky - Bratislava -
  - Brno - Prague

RailJet (RJX)
- Bratislava - Vienna - Salzburg -
  Innsbruck - Zurich

SuperCity (SC)
- Kosice - Poprad - Zilina -
  Ostrava - Prague

InterCity (IC)

- Kosice - Poprad - Zilina -
  Ostrava - Prague
- Kosice - Poprad - Zilina -
  Bratislava - Vienna

Regional trains to Vienna (REX)

- REX 6: Bratislava Petrzalka -
  Bruck an der Leitha - Vienna
- REX 8: Bratislava Hl. St. - Devinska Nova Ves - Vienna

LEO Express

- International train runs between Slovakia and the Czech Republic. This train requires an Interrail Global Pass or a Slovakia Pass to board.
- Reservations are free, however, they must be made before boarding.
- Tickets may be reserved up to three months in advance on the website leoexpress.com.
- Routes available:
  - Kosice - Poprad - Zilina -
    Ostrava - Olomouc - Prague

RegioJet

- International trains connect Slovakia with the Czech Republic. This train requires an Interrail Global Pass or a Slovakia Pass to board.
- Most trains need reservations.
- Tickets may be reserved up to three months in advance on the website regioet.com.
- Reservations are required on the following (RJ) routes:
  - Kosice - Poprad - Zilina -
    Ostrava - Olomouc - Prague
  - Kosice - Poprad - Zilina -
    Ostrava - Olomouc - Prague (night train)
  - Bratislava - Brno - Prague
  - Prague to Rijeka seasonal direct trains from are not included.
    (RJ 1044/1047/1367/1364)

Night Trains

Night trains go from Slovakia to the Czech Republic, Poland, Germany, and Croatia.

Domestic Night Trains

- Bratislava - Zilina - Poprad - Kosice - Humenne (R 615 Zemplin)
- Bratislava - Nove Zamky - Zvolen - Kosice (R 801 Pol'ana)

EuroNight (EN)

- Kosice - Poprad - Ostrava - Prague
- Humenne - Kosice - Poprad - Ostrava - Prague
- Kosice - Zvolen - Bratislava - Brno - Prague
- Budapest - Bratislava - Breclav - Brno - Prague
- Budapest - Bratislava - Breclav - Krakow - Warsaw
- Budapest - Bratislava - Breclav - Ostrava - Wroclaw - Berlin
- Bratislava - Vienna - Maribor - Zagreb - Split (summer only)

RegioJet (RJ)

- Kosice - Poprad - Zilina - - Ostrava - Olomouc - Prague

Popular connections

Domestic routes

Let me show you the typical travel times between Slovakia's major cities. Reservations are not required for any of these train itineraries.

Route	Travel time (by InterCity)
Bratislava to Kosice	4h 50m
Bratislava to Presov	5h 20m
Bratislava to Zilina	1h 45m
Bratislava to Poprad (Tatra Mountains)	3h 30m
Bratislava to Banska Bystrica	3h 40m

International Routes

Route	Which train?	Travel Time	Reservations
Bratislava to Berlin (Germany)	EuroNight	10h 10m	required
Bratislava to Budapest (Hungary)	EuroCity	2h 40m	Optional
Bratislava to Prague (Czech Republic)	EuroCity / RegioJet	4h	Required (EuroCity) / Optional (RegioJet)

Bratislava to Vienna (Austria)	Regional	1h	not necessary.
Bratislava to Warsaw (Poland)	EuroNight	8h	Required

Reservations

Train bookings in Slovakia:

Eurail reservation self-service system

- Eurail
  - R, EX, IC, EC, SC, RailJet, Nightjet, Euro Night

Administration fees when booking via Eurail self-service

- EUR 2,- per person per train
- Additional € 9,- per order
  (for paper tickets)

With railway carriers

- ZSSK (Slovakian Railways): Domestic and international trains
  - RailJet, IC, EC, NightJet, EuroNight

- CD (Czech railways): Domestic and international trains
  - RailJet, IC, EC, NightJet, EuroNight

- ŌBB (Austrian railways):
  (Some domestic and) International trains
  - RailJet, IC, EC, NightJet, and EuroNight

- Leo Express: Only local and international Leo Express trains
- RegioJet: Only local and international RegioJet trains operate.

Slovakia Pass

- Spend your whole holiday discovering Slovakia by train.
- Standard pricing begins at $ 59.

Global Pass

- You are free to visit Slovakia and up to 32 other European countries.
- Standard pricing begins at $ 211.

Slovakia Tips & Tricks

Quick facts

- Bratislava is the capital of Slovakia.
- Population: 5.4 million
- Slovak is the language.
- Euro (EUR)
- +421 is the dialing code.

Slovakia's principal rail station

Slovakia's railway hub is in Bratislava

- Bratislava Hlavna Stanica (main station)
- It features ticket machines and an information service.
- 1 km from Bratislava's Old Town.
- There are bus and tram stops, Outside the station.

Hotels and resorts

In Slovakia, holders of Eurail passes get discounts on accommodation at a variety of hotels and wellness centers.

Serbia

The train is an excellent method to visit Serbia and its capital, Belgrade. Serbia is well-known for its magnificent landscape, historical history, curative spas, and diverse flora and wildlife. Step aboard and discover a place unlike any other.

Routes Map

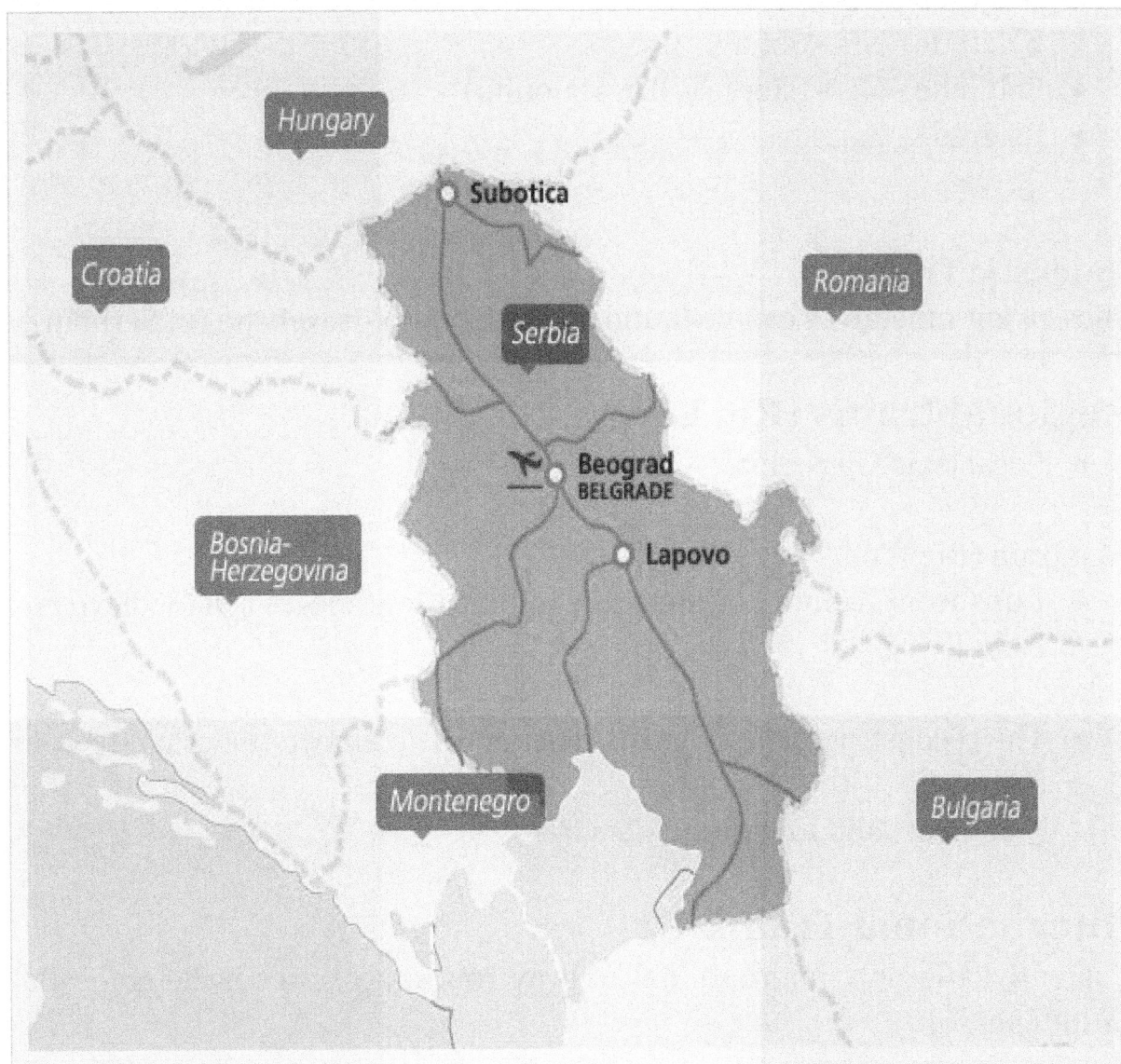

Train types in Serbia

Serbian Railways (ZS) operates trains throughout the country.

Train schedules can be found on the Srbija Voz website (in Serbian). w3.srbvoz.rs

Please note that the following train services are presently suspended due to infrastructure work:
- Novi Sad - Subotica - Kelebia - Budapest
- Belgrade - Budapest
- Belgrade - Nis - Sofia
- Belgrade - Nis - Skopje (- Thessaloniki)
- Belgrade - Zagreb

Domestic Trains
These train timetables can be found on the Srbija Voz website (in Serbian).

Regional trains (Re, REx)
- Local trains in Serbia

Fast train (Brzi Voz)
- Runs from Zemun and Belgrade to Bar (Montenegro), via Valjevo and Priboj.

Soko
- The reconstructed 200 km/h railway line connects Belgrade to Novi Sad.
  - Not valid for passholders

International Trains
Currently, the only international railway route in service is Belgrade-Bar (Montenegro).

Fast train (Brzi Voz)
- Zemun - Beograd Centar -
  Valjevo - Priboj - Podgorica - Bar
- Reservations must be made.
- Seasonal: June 16th to September 17th

Night Trains

Currently, the only international railway route in service is Belgrade-Bar (Montenegro).

Fast train (Brzi Voz)
- Zemun - Beograd Centar -
- Valjevo - Priboj - Podgorica - Bar
- This category includes seats, couchettes/berths, and sleepers.
- Reservations must be made.

You can take your bike on the train. You must pay a price of 100 dinars (about $ 0.85 USD) and park your bike in one of the authorized bike places aboard the train. provided the train does not have any designated bike areas, you are permitted to bring your bike provided it can be folded and stored as a luggage item. More information may be found on the Serbian Railways website.

Popular connections
Domestic Routes

Time it takes to travel between cities in Serbia. The typical travel times are shown in the table below.

Route	Travel time
Belgrade to Nis	6h

Belgrade to Novi Sad (via Re regional train, Soko trains are not included)	1h

International Routes

Routes	Which train?	Travel time	Reservations
Belgrade to Bar (Montenegro)	11h scenic day/night train required		

Many railway lines are now under development, therefore there are no direct trains from Belgrade to Budapest, Zagreb, Sofia, or Skopje.

Reservations

How to Book Train Tickets in Serbia
- locally at the train station

Which trains in Serbia need reservations?
- International Express trains (EXP) cost around €3 (RZD 350 in local currency).

Serbia Pass

- Spend your whole trip visiting Serbia by train.
- Standard pricing starts at € 59.

Global Pass

- You are free to visit Serbia and up to 32 other European countries.
- Prices start at € 211.

Serbian Tips & Tricks

Serbian Railway Museum in Belgrade
Those with a valid Eurail pass for Serbia can enter this railway museum for free.

Quick Facts

- Capital: Belgrade (Beograd, spelled Београд)
- Population: 7.2 million
- Language: Serbian
- Serbian Dinar (RSD)
- +381: dialing code.

Eurail Help Office

If you have any questions concerning Eurail, you can visit the international ticket office at Beograd train station (Belgrade), which is open 24 hours.

Airport train station connections

From the International Airport Nikola Tesla, take bus 72 to the bus stop Zeleni Venac (approximately 500m (0.3 km) from Belgrade's train station). Eurail passes are not valid on this route.

Slovenia

Your Eurail Pass is your ticket to an unforgettable rail experience. Slovenia's magnificent architecture, mountain landscapes, and gorgeous Adriatic coast await you. There are several Eurail passes to select from if you wish to visit this intriguing and beautiful country by rail. The comfort and efficiency of rail travel will make it well worth your time.

Routes Map

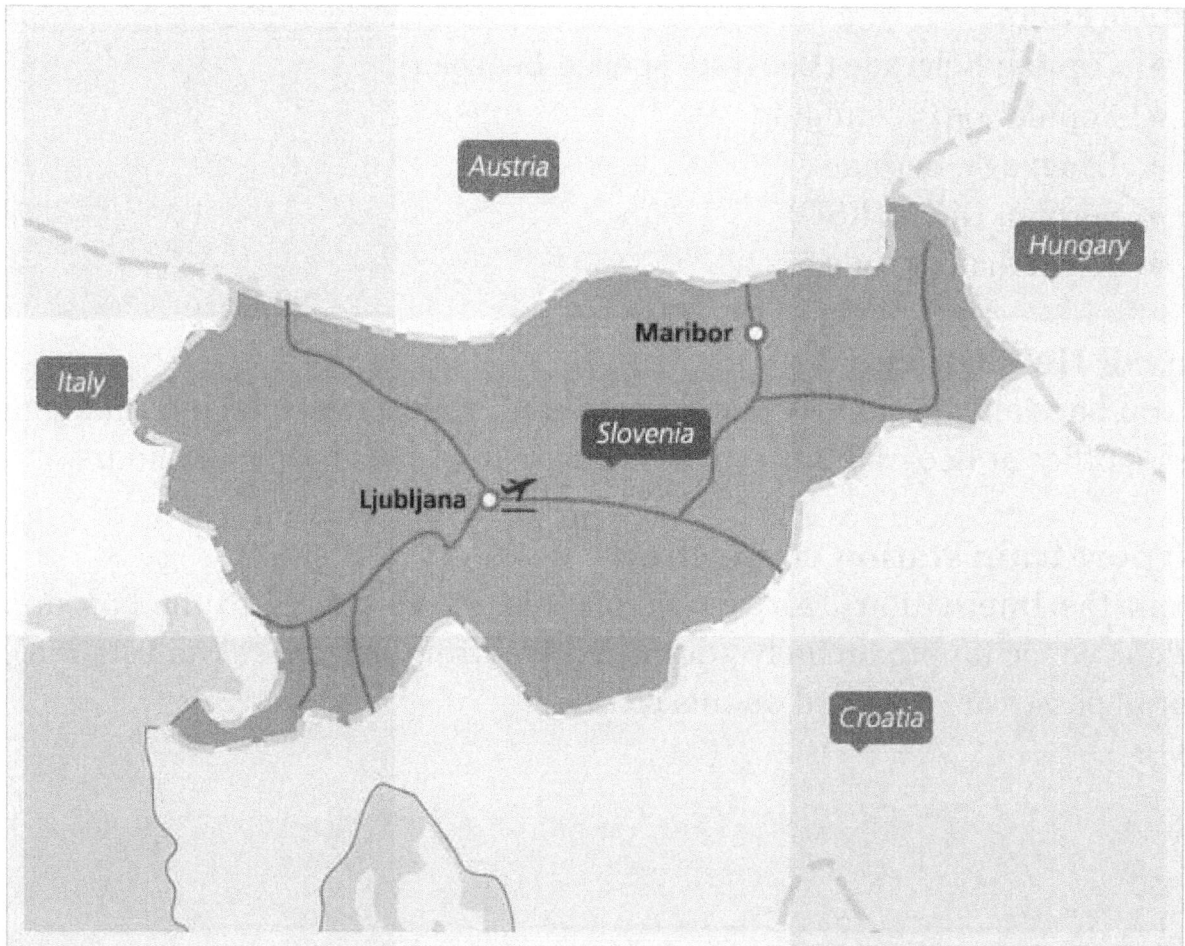

Train types

Rail Network

Slovenia's national railway company is named SZ (Slovenian Railways - Slovenske zeleznice).

How to Get There

Ljubljana, Slovenia's capital, is easily accessible by direct trains from Austria (Vienna), Germany (Munich), Switzerland (Zurich), Croatia (Zagreb), Hungary (Budapest), and Serbia (Belgrade).

Regional and intercity trains in Slovenia

Regionalni vlaki (RE)

- Regional trains connect bigger cities to smaller towns and villages.
- Only 2nd class carriages are available.
- Bicycles are permitted on board with the purchase of a specific bike ticket.
- There is no need for a reservation.

Lokalni potniski (RE)

- Local trains travel on suburban commuter lines.
- Only 2nd class carriages are available.
- There is no need for a reservation.

InterCity (IC)

- Slovenia's largest towns and cities are linked by fast trains.
- Bicycles are permitted on board with the purchase of a specific bike ticket.
- Reservations are not necessary, however, they may be beneficial if traveling during a busy season.

InterCitySlovenija (PEN)

- Tilting, rapid pendolino trains provide the finest comfort and rail experience in Slovenia.
- Regular services between Maribor and Ljubljana.
- A seat reservation is not required, although it may be worthwhile if you are going during a busy season.

International Trains in Slovenia

EuroCity (EC)

- Fast, modern trains link Slovenia's main cities with the rest of Europe.
- The following services are offered to/from Slovenia:
- Trieste - Ljubljana - Maribor - Graz - Vienna
- Zagreb - Ljubljana - Villach - Salzburg - Munich - Frankfurt am Main

InterCity (IC)

- Fast trains link Slovenia's largest cities with the rest of Europe.
- The following services are offered to/from Slovenia:
- Vinkovci - Zagreb - Ljubljana - Villach
- Ljubljana - Graz - Budapest
- Ljubljana - Budapest
- Ljubljana - Rijeka
- Ljubljana - Villach

Night trains in Slovenia

EuroNight (EN)

- International night train linking Slovenia with Austria, Croatia, Germany, and Switzerland.
- The following services are offered to/from Slovenia:
    - Ljubljana - Zurich

○ Ljubljana - Munich - Stuttgart

Connection from the airport to the city

You can take a bus from the International Airport to the Ljubljana train station. The trip takes roughly 45 minutes. Eurail passes are not valid on this route.

Eurail Assistance Office

You can get support with Eurail in Slovenia by visiting the international ticket office at:

Ljubljana Railway Station

- Mon-Fri: 08.00 - 20.00
- Saturday, Sunday, and holidays are all closed.

Popular connections

Domestic Routes

Route	Travel time
Ljubljana to Maribor	1h 45m
Ljubljana to Koper	2h 30m
Ljubljana to Celje	1h 05m
Ljubljana to Lesce-Bled (take the bus to Lake Bled)	50m
Ljubljana to Bled Jezero (train via Jesenice)	1h 30m

International routes

Travel to and from Slovenia is possible from the following prominent European cities:

Route	Train type	Duration	Reservations
Ljubljana to Budapest (Hungary)	InterCity	7h 25m	Optional
Ljubljana to Munich (Germany)	EuroCity	6h 15m	Optional
Ljubljana to Villach (Austria)	EuroCity	1h 40m	Optional
Ljubljana to Zagreb (Croatia)	EuroCity	2h 10m	Optional
Ljubljana to Zurich (Switzerland)	EuroNight	11h 10m (overnight)	Required
Maribor to Graz (Austria)	EuroCity	1h	Optional
Ljubljana to Trieste (Italy)	EuroCity	2h 55m	Optional

Reservations

How do I book train tickets in Slovenia?

Reservation system for Eurail
- Eurail

Administration fees when booking through Eurail self-service:
- € 2,- per person per train
- Additional € 9,- per order
  (for paper tickets)

With railway carriers
- ÖBB (Austrian Railways):
  Domestic and international trains

locally at the train station

Which trains in Slovenia require reservations?
- Regional trains (RE) and Interregio (IR) do not require reservations.
- Trains InterCity, EuroCity, and Pendolino are optional.
- Reservations are highly recommended, however during the summer season.
- EuroNight is mandatory on all routes.

Slovenia Pass

- Spend your entire vacation discovering Slovenia by rail.
- Standard prices begin at $ 59.

Global Pass

- Explore Slovenia and up to 32 other European countries.
- Standard prices begin at $ 211.

Tricks and Tips

Slovenian Pass Benefits

Travel by bus is completely free.

A valid Eurail pass in Slovenia entitles you to free travel on the following bus routes:

- Divaca - SKocjan Caves

Hotel and resort services

Eurail pass holders also receive discounts on swimming pools, aqua parks, and saunas at various hotels and wellness spas.

Station Facilities

Stations in Slovenia typically have excellent facilities such as:

- Luggage lockers
- Foreign exchange desks
- Restaurants and cafés
- Tourist information offices
- ATM cash machines
- Elevators and escalators
- Access for passengers with disabilities

Quick facts

- Capital: Ljubljana
- Population: 2 million
- Slovene: language.
- Euro (EUR): Currency
- +386: dialing code.

Slovenian hub stations

Slovenia's main train stations are as follows:

- Ljubljana Central Train Station
- Maribor Train Station (eleznika postaja Maribor)
- Celje Train Station

Switzerland

Many European travelers want to visit Switzerland. With a Eurail Pass, you can travel through the snow-capped Alps, alongside beautiful mountain lakes, and across rolling green hills. Switzerland's beautiful scenery and charming cities make it a must-see destination.

Routes Map

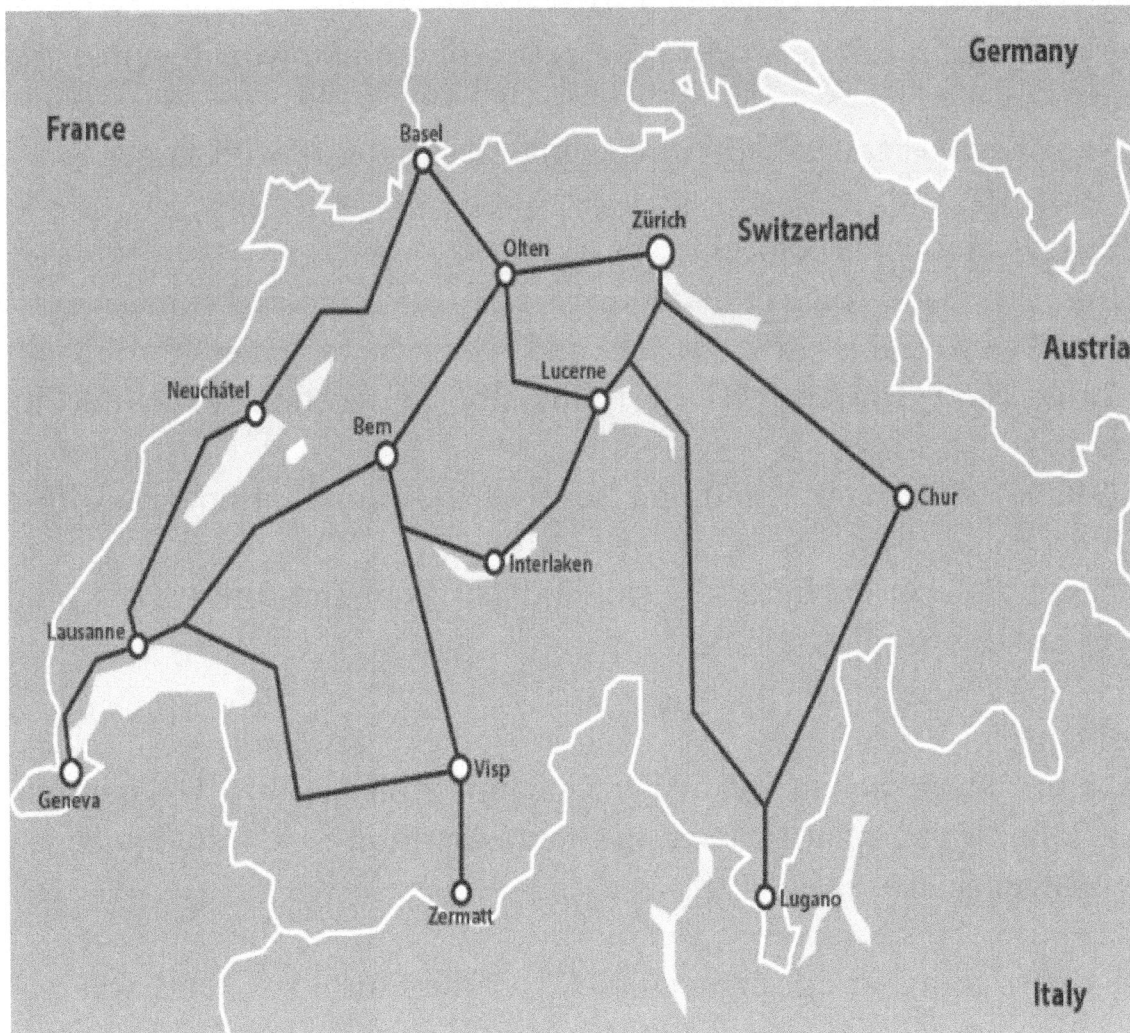

Train types in Switzerland

Switzerland has a variety of train types available to transport you across the country as well as to and from other European countries at all hours of the day and night.

The SBB (Schweizerische BundesBahn) is Switzerland's national railway company.

To check train times in Switzerland, visit eurail.com or the SBB timetable at www.sbb.ch/en.

Regional trains in Switzerland

Switzerland's main rail network is comprised of the following regional and intercity trains:

- RegioExpress trains connect regional destinations with larger Swiss cities.
- Regio trains connect local towns.
- InterCity trains connect major Swiss cities such as Basel and Geneva.
- InterRegio trains link Zurich and Geneva to cities throughout Switzerland. However, These trains stop more often than InterCity trains.
- S-Bahn (suburban trains) is a network of trains that operate within most major cities.
- Zurich: Except for lines S4, S10, and S18, your Interrail Pass is valid on Zurich's S-bahn.

Travel tip:

There is an international regional train connection between Chiasso and Milan (Italy). If you want to avoid paying reservation fees, this connection is an excellent choice.

RegioExpress trains are designated "RE" on the Eurail schedule, whereas Regio trains are labeled "R". InterCity trains are labeled as "IC," whereas InterRegio trains are designated as "IR." Regional and intercity trains do not need seat reservations. Reservations are strongly advised for intercity trains during peak season (May-September) and on public holidays.

Switzerland has high-speed trains.

International high-speed trains in Switzerland
These high-speed trains travel to and from Switzerland:

- ICE connects Switzerland to cities in Germany and the Netherlands.
- Basel - Frankfurt - Cologne - Hamburg
- Basel - Stuttgart - Munich
- Basel - Frankfurt - Cologne - Amsterdam
  - Reservations are required during the summer season (June 17th through August 18th).
  - Basel-Amsterdam trains will only run until Düsseldorf between May 27th and September 12th.
  - Interlaken - Basel - Frankfurt - Berlin
  - Zürich - Basel - Frankfurt - Hannover - Hamburg - Kiel

- Railjet (RJX) connects Zurich to cities in Austria, Slovakia, and Hungary.
  - Zürich - Salzburg - Vienna - Bratislava/Budapest

- EuroCity (EC) connects Zurich, Basel, and Geneva to cities in Italy, Austria, the Czech Republic, and Germany.
  - Zürich - Innsbruck - Graz
  - Interlaken/Zürich - Basel - Cologne - Hamburg
  - Zürich - Milan - Genova/Bologna/Verona/Venezia
  - Geneva - Lausanne - Milan
  - Basel - Bern - Luzern - Milan
  - Zürich - Frankfurt - Dresden - Prague (Overnight)

InterCity (IC)
- connects Zurich to cities in the Netherlands and Germany.
  - Zürich - Stuttgart
  - Zürich - Frankfurt - Hamburg (overnight)
  - Zürich - Frankfurt - Amsterdam (overnight)
  - Zürich - Frankfurt - Berlin (overnight)

EuroCityExpress (ECE).
- Zurich is connected to cities in Germany and Italy
  - Frankfurt - Basel - Milan
  - Zürich - Munich

TGV trains connect Zurich, Basel, Geneva, and Lausanne to Paris (France).
- Zürich - Basel - Paris
- Lausanne - Geneva - Paris
- Lausanne - Dijon - Paris
- Geneva - Lyon - Marseille (only from July 1 to August 27)

Domestic high-speed trains in Switzerland
InterCity Neigezug (ICN) refers to Swiss domestic high-speed trains. ICN trains transport passengers quickly and comfortably from one end of the country to the other.

Night trains in and out of Switzerland
International night trains
The following night trains connect Switzerland to Austria, Germany, Hungary, Croatia, Czechia, Slovenia, and the Netherlands:
- ÖBB Nightjet:
  - Zurich - Basel - Hamburg
  - Zurich - Basel - Düsseldorf - Amsterdam
  - Zurich - Basel - Berlin
  - Zurich - Linz - Vienna

- EuroNight:
  - Zurich - Graz
  - Zurich - Vienna - Budapest
  - Zurich - Innsbruck - Prague
  - Zurich - Basel - Dresden - Prague
  - Zurich - Villach - Ljubljana - Zagreb

Switzerland's scenic train routes

Switzerland is well-known for its breathtaking scenery. The scenic train routes listed below offer special conditions for Eurail pass holders:

- Bernina Express: Chur-Lugano via Tirano (Italy)
- Chocolate train: Montreux - Broc-Chocolat
- Centovalli Railway: Locarno (Switzerland) - Domodossola (Italy)
- Golden Pass: Luzern - Interlaken - Montreux
- Glacier Express: Davos/St. Moritz - Zermatt

Popular connections
Domestic Routes

Route	Travel time
Basel to Bern	55m
Basel to Interlaken	2h
Basel to Lucerne	1h

Basel to Zurich	55m
Bern to Geneva	1h 45m
Bern to Interlaken	55m
Bern to Zurich	55m
Geneva to Zurich	2h 45m
Zurich to Lugano	1h 55m
Bern to Brig	1h 05m

International Routes

Route	Which train?	Travel time	Reservations
Zurich to Graz / Villach (Austria)	EuroNight	10h 55m (overnight) / 10h 05m (overnight)	Required
Zurich to Hamburg (Germany)	ICE / ÖBB Nightjet	7h 35m / 11h 35m (overnight)	Optional / Required
Zurich to Vienna (Austria)	RailJet / EuroNight	7h 50m / 8h 55m (overnight)	Optional / Required
Zurich / Basel / Geneva to Paris (France)	TGV Lyria	4h / 3h / 3h	Required
Zurich / Bern / Geneva to Milan (Italy)	EuroCity	4h / 3h / 4h	Required
Zürich to Amsterdam (the Netherlands)	IC + ICE / ÖBB Nightjet	6h 45m / 12h (overnight)	Optional / Required

Zürich to Prague (Czechia)	EuroNight	13h (overnight)	Required
Zürich to Munich (Germany)	EuroCity	3h 30m	Optional
Zürich to Cologne	ICE / EuroCity	5h / 6h	Optional

Reservations

Reservations for SBB regional trains are not required. Reservations are not required for InterCity and ICN trains, but we recommend that you do so during the busy summer season (May - September) and on public holidays. However, Reservations are required for night trains and international high-speed trains. The cost of a night train depends on the type of sleeping accommodation you select.

Reservations for Swiss trains

Reservations can be made for domestic and international high-speed trains, as well as night trains:

- Using our Reservation Service.
- Online at the SBB website. www.sbb.ch/en
- At a ticket counter or self-service machine at a local train station.
- By phone, contact the SBB Contact Center.
  - +41 848 44 66 88
  - Availability: 24/7

When you call this booking center, you will be connected directly. The Swiss SBB booking center can deliver your reservations to any European country. The delivery fee is CHF8 (approx. €6.50). However, This call center can charge a booking fee. You can also pick up your reservations at major Swiss train stations. Simply bring your order number to the box office.

Switzerland Pass

Global Pass

- Feel free to visit Switzerland and the other 32 European countries.
- Standard prices begin at $ 211.

Tricks and Tips

Quick facts

- Switzerland: Berne
- Population: 8 million
- Languages: German, French, and Italian
- Swiss Franc (CHF)
- dialing code: +41

Swiss hub stations

Switzerland's main hub stations are Basel SBB, Bern, Geneva, Lausanne, Luzern, and Zürich HB, from which trains to most of the country's major cities can be connected.

Station Facilities

Stations in Switzerland typically have excellent facilities, which often include:

- Luggage storage

- Foreign exchange desks
- Restaurants and cafés
- Tourist information offices
- ATM cash machines
- Elevators and escalators
- Shops
- Access for passengers with disabilities

The spelling of city names

The local spelling of Swiss cities and stations is usually found on Swiss train timetables and at Swiss train stations.

Here is the local spelling of some well-known Swiss cities:

- Geneva = Genève
- Lucerne = Luzern

Sweden

Sweden is a fascinating and attractive place to visit. From charming cities like Stockholm to seemingly endless natural wonders, your Eurail Sweden Pass will show you the best of what this country has to offer. The views from the train, as well as the stops along the way, will create memories that will last a lifetime.

Routes Map

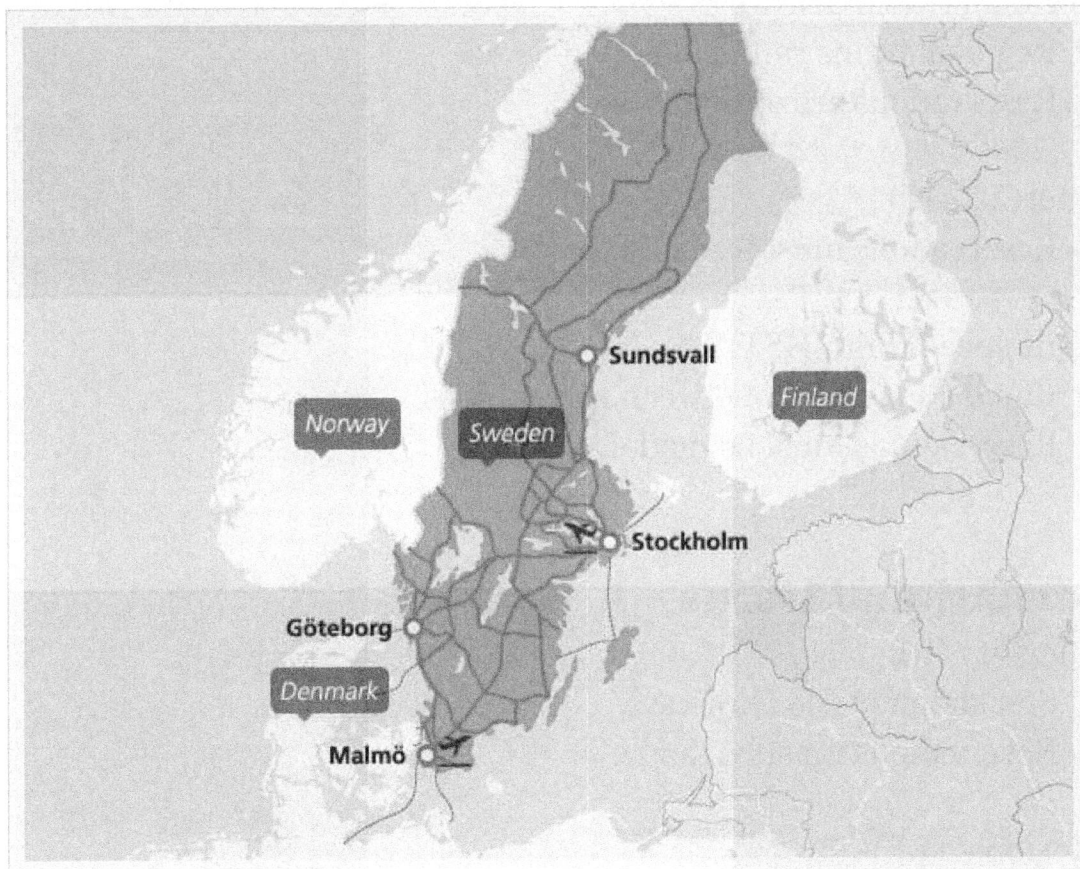

Train types in Sweden

SJ operates the extensive Swedish railway network. Modern trains travel between cities in Sweden on a regular basis, providing both comfort and breathtaking views from the train window. Swedish train times can be found in the Eurail timetable.

Bicycles are not permitted on Swedish trains unless they are foldable and can be carried as hand luggage.

Domestic Trains

SJ Regional (REGIONAL)
- Regional trains run throughout Sweden.
- Reservations are optional.

SJ InterCity (IC)
- Reservations must be made.

SJ High-speed train (HST)
- Rapid connectivity between major cities
- Reservations must be made.

International trains

SJ InterCity (IC)
- Stockholm - Oslo (Norway)
- Reservations must be made.

VY Regional (RE)
- Göteborg - Oslo (Norway)
- Reservations are optional.

SJ High Speed (HST)
- Stockholm - Copenhagen (Denmark)

- Reservations must be made.

Öresundstg trains (regional)
- Malmö - Copenhagen (Denmark)
- Reservations are optional.

Night trains
Reservations are required for all night trains.
SJ night train (NT)
- Domestic routes within Sweden
    - Stockholm - östersund - re - duved (ski resorts)
    - Göteborg - stersund - re - Duved (ski resorts)
    - Stockholm - Umeå
    - Göteborg - Umeå
    - Stockholm to Malmö

SJ EuroNight
- Stockholm - Malmö - Copenhagen Airport - Hamburg (Altona) - Berlin (beginning in April 2023)

VY night train
- Stockholm - Boden - Kiruna - Narvik (Norway)
- Stockholm - Boden - Lule

Snälltåget night train
- Malmö - Stockholm - stersund - re - Duved - Storlien (ski resorts)
- Stockholm - Malmö - Copenhagen restad - Hamburg - Berlin

Scenic Trains
Inlandsbanan
- Travels all the way to the Arctic Circle

- Your Eurail Pass includes everything you need.

Iron Ore Line
- Across the Arctic Circle, from Lule to Narvik
- From the Gulf of Bothnia to the Atlantic Ocean
- Your Eurail pass covers trains on this line operated by VY Norrtg.

Popular connections

Domestic routes

These are the average travel times between Sweden's major cities. Reservations are not required for any of these train journeys.

Route	Travel time
Stockholm to Gothenburgq	3h
Stockholm to Kiruna (Night train via Sundsvall)	17h 30m
Stockholm to Malmö	4h 30m
Stockholm to Sundsvall	3h 50m

International routes

Route	Which train?	Travel time	Reservations
Stockholm to Copenhagen (Denmark)	SJ high-speed	5h 05m	Required
Stockholm	SJ high-speed +	10h 40m	Required

(via Copenhagen, Denmark) to Hamburg (Germany)	InterCity		
Stockholm to Oslo (Norway)	SJ high-speed	5h 30m	Required
Göteborg to Oslo (Norway)	Regional	3h 30m	Recommended
Stockholm to Berlin (Germany)	SJ EuroNight / Snälltaget	15h 30m (overnight)	Required

Reservations

Reservation system for Eurail
- Eurail
- RE, IC, HST (X2000), domestic night trains,
- EuroNight, Snälltaget

Booking through Eurail self-service administrative fees cost.
- € 2,- per person per train
- Additional € 9,- per order
  (for paper tickets)

With railway carriers
- SJ (Swedish Railways): Domestic and international trains
- X2000, IC
- Snälltåget: Only domestic and international Snälltaget trains operate.
- DB (German Railways): International trips to Germany via Denmark
  - IC

Sweden Pass

Use your entire vacation to explore Sweden by train. Standard prices begin at $ 169.

Global Pass

- Explore Sweden and up to 32 other European countries.
- Standard prices begin at $ 211.

Scandinavia Pass

- Travel by train through Finland, Denmark, Sweden, and Norway.
- Standard prices start at $ 190.

Sweden Tips and Tricks

Quick facts

- Stockholm: Capital
- Population: 9.5 million
- Language: Swedish
- Swedish Krona (SEK)
- Dialing code: +46

The spelling of city names

The local spelling of Swedish cities and stations can usually be found on Swedish train timetables and at Swedish train stations. Here is the local spelling of some well-known Swedish cities:

- Gothenburg = Göteborg

Discounts on ferry tickets and other services

With a valid Eurail Pass for Sweden, you can save money on ferry tickets to the following countries:

- Finland
- Estonia
- Latvia
- Germany

A valid Eurail Pass in Sweden entitles you to unlimited travel on the following routes:

- SJ trains run directly to and from Copenhagen, as well as to Copenhagen Airport.
- From Göteborg and Stockholm to Oslo.

Europe Train Trip for Foodies

2 weeks in Europe for Foodies

Eat your way across the finest cuisine cities! During these two weeks in Europe, you'll see three countries, and six cities, and sample innumerable delicacies. This schedule is designed for persons who consider food to be an important component of the cultural experience.

Short itinerary

Cities visited on this trip:

1. Paris, France
2. San Sebastián, Spain
3. Barcelona, Spain
4. Lyon, France
5. Bologna, Italy
6. Rome, Italy

For this journey, I recommend:

- Eurail Pass: Global Pass
- Travel days: 7 days within a month

Paris, France

• Macarons in Paris, France

Fine dining was mastered in Paris. The French capital boasts the most Michelin stars of any city in Europe!

From croissants and baguettes to macarons and crêpes, French snacks are available throughout the city.

Feeling daring? Fill up on protein with escargots, which are sautéed snails with garlic butter.

The Parisian metro will transport you from the major airport to the city center in 15 minutes.

San Sebastián, Spain

The old town is packed with pintxos eateries. Note, Pintxo that are tapas served on a skewer or toothpick.

The colorful subterranean La Bretxa Market is where the region's greatest chefs go to acquire top-quality seasonal fruit.

Still hungry? Join a cooking class for hands-on instruction in the art of Basque food.

Take the train from Paris to Hendaye (France), then a bus or tram to Irun (Spain), then a train to San Sebastián (reservation necessary).

Barcelona, Spain

Barcelona, Spain

Tapas are served on popular terraces in Barcelona, such as Plaça Reial. Local favorites include fish and pork.

Explore the labyrinth of food vendors at La Boqueria Market, which is located right off the pedestrian boulevard La Rambla.

You can also sample specialties from other Spanish towns, such as gazpacho (Seville) and paella (Valencia).

Direct trains from San Sebastián take less than 6 hours. Reservations are necessary.

Lyon, France

Lyon is the world's gourmet capital! Local dishes include duck pâté, sausages, and roast pig.

Dine at bouchons, which are classic Lyonnaise restaurants. Authentic bouchons are properly certified.

Lyon's major market, Halles de Lyon Paul Bocuse, is packed with fresh local food and French delicacies.

A direct train from Barcelona to Lyon takes 5 hours (reservations necessary).

Bologna, Italy

The Quadrilatero is the pulsing heart of Bologna's cuisine scene. The bustling market is packed with food stands.

Dine at an osteria, a tiny restaurant with short menus and regional delicacies. Bologna has Italy's oldest osteria.

When in Bologna, have your pasta with Bolognese sauce! Simply order the tagliatelle al ragù.

Train travel from Lyon to Bologna takes around 7 hours (reservation necessary).

Rome, Italy

Do you crave pizza? Restaurants in the tourist district should be avoided. The tastiest pizzerias can be discovered in quiet alleys.

Start with bruschetta and finish with pasta carbonara for a classic Roman meal.

True pasta enthusiasts should visit the National Museum of Pasta (Museo Nazionale della Paste Alimentari).

Regular direct trains from Bologna to Rome take slightly over 2 hours (reservations necessary).

Things I Wish I Had Understood Before Taking Eurail to Europe

As a seasoned traveler, I've had my fair share of adventures, but nothing quite prepared me for the grand tour of Europe by Eurail. While the experience was undeniably enriching, there were a few things I wish I had understood beforehand. Here's a glimpse into my European escapade, complete with some hard-earned insights.

1. Embrace the Unexpected

Europe is a continent brimming with surprises, and Eurail is your ticket to unlocking them. Don't be afraid to veer off the beaten path and explore the hidden gems that lie just beyond the well-trodden tourist routes. The quaint villages, local markets, and off-the-menu dining experiences often hold the most authentic and memorable moments.

2. Expect Delays and Be Flexible

Train travel in Europe is generally efficient and reliable, but delays are not uncommon. Embrace this as part of the adventure and learn to roll with the punches. If your train is running late, don't panic. Instead, use the extra time to grab a coffee, people-watch, or soak up the local atmosphere.

3. Pack Light and Smart

Lugging heavy suitcases through train stations and up steep city streets is no fun. Pack light and smart, bringing only essentials and versatile pieces that can be mixed and matched. Remember, you'll be doing a lot of walking, so comfortable shoes are a must.

4. Embrace the Slow Travel Philosophy

Eurail is not about ticking off destinations in a checklist; it's about savoring the journey. Slow down, immerse yourself in the local culture, and appreciate the little things. Take time to linger over a cup of coffee in a sidewalk café, wander through a bustling market, or simply sit on a park bench and watch the world go by.

5. Learn a Few Basic Phrases

While English is widely spoken in major tourist areas, learning a few basic phrases in the local language will go a long way in enhancing your experience. You'll be surprised how much more warmth and appreciation you receive when you make an effort to communicate in their language.

6. Be Prepared for Different Train Types

Eurail offers a variety of train types, each with its own amenities and comfort levels. From high-speed intercity trains to slower regional trains, each serves a different purpose. Research the different train options and choose the ones that best suit your itinerary and budget.

7. Embrace the Spontaneity

The beauty of Eurail travel lies in its spontaneity. Don't be afraid to change your plans if an unexpected opportunity arises.

8. Connect with Fellow Travelers

Strike up conversations, share stories, and learn about their perspectives. These encounters will enrich your journey and create lasting memories.

9. Savor the Local Cuisine

Europe is a culinary paradise, with each region boasting its own unique flavors and traditions. Venture beyond the tourist traps and seek out local restaurants and markets. Try the regional specialties, sample local wines, and indulge in the culinary delights that each city has to offer.

10. Embrace the Challenge

Traveling by Eurail can be challenging at times, but that's part of it's charm.

Enjoy Your Tour

TRAVEL JOURNAL

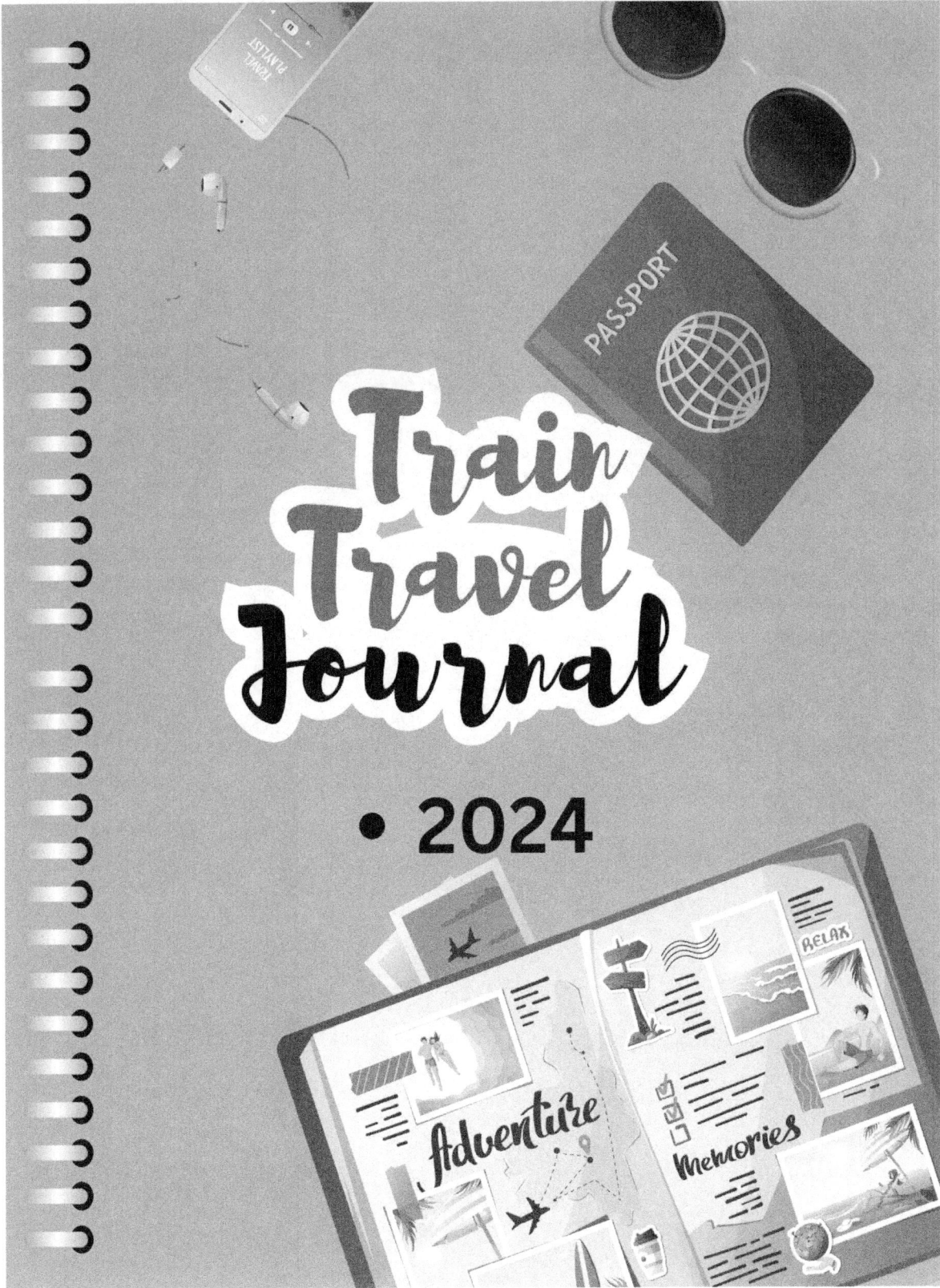

Date:

Location:

Budget:

KINDS OF TRANSPORTATION:

_____

_____

_____

My Travel Planner

Personal Itinerary

TODAY'S LOG

6 AM	
7 AM	
8 AM	
9 AM	
10 AM	
11 AM	
12 PM	
1 PM	
2 PM	
3 PM	
4 PM	
5 PM	
6 PM	

PLACES TO GO

LOCAL FOODS TO TRY

_____

_____

_____

REMINDER

Packing list

Item	✔

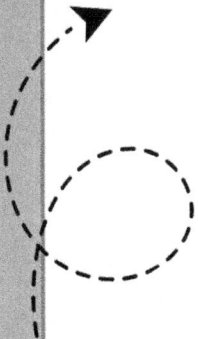

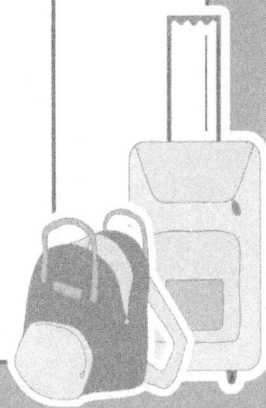

✈ TRAVEL ITINERARY

Destination:	Duration:
Arrival:	Departure:

Hotel Address:

Transportation:

Day 1

Time	Activity
8:00 am	
12:00 nn	
1:00 pm	
3:00 pm	
7:00 pm	
10:00 pm	

Day 2

Time	Activity
8:00 am	
12:00 nn	
1:00 pm	
3:00 pm	
7:00 pm	
10:00 pm	

Day 3

Time	Activity
8:00 am	
12:00 nn	
1:00 pm	
3:00 pm	
7:00 pm	
10:00 pm	

Day 4

Time	Activity
8:00 am	
12:00 nn	
1:00 pm	
3:00 pm	
7:00 pm	
10:00 pm	

Day 5

Time	Activity
8:00 am	
12:00 nn	
1:00 pm	
3:00 pm	
7:00 pm	
10:00 pm	

Day 6

Time	Activity
8:00 am	
12:00 nn	
1:00 pm	
3:00 pm	
7:00 pm	
10:00 pm	

Day 7

Time	Activity
8:00 am	
12:00 nn	
1:00 pm	
3:00 pm	
7:00 pm	
10:00 pm	

Day 8

Time	Activity
8:00 am	
12:00 nn	
1:00 pm	
3:00 pm	
7:00 pm	
10:00 pm	

Day 9

Time	Activity
8:00 am	
12:00 nn	
1:00 pm	
3:00 pm	
7:00 pm	
10:00 pm	

Experiences

PREPARATION AND NOTES

I will do:

I will do:

I will do:

I will do:

I will do:

I WANTED TO DO THESE

Because...

_____

_____

_____

_____

_____

_____

_____

_____

_____

_____

_____

_____

_____

_____

Travel Adventures

ACCOMPLISHED

Bucket List

- [ ]
- [ ]
- [ ]
- [ ]
- [ ]
- [ ]
- [ ]

How do you feel about accomplishing your list

_____

_____

_____

_____

_____

_____

_____

_____

Printed in Great Britain
by Amazon